THE REFORMATORY

AT

MOUNT ST BERNARD ABBEY

1856-1881

MAUREEN HAVERS

MOUNT ST BERNARD ABBEY

Published by Mount St Bernard Abbey
Oaks Road
Coalville
Leicestershire
LE67 5UL

All rights reserved. No part of this publication may be reproduced, stored in a retrieval system, or transmitted in any form, or by any means, electronic, mechanical, photocopying, recording or otherwise, without the written permission of the publisher.

Copyright Mount St Bernard Abbey
ISBN 0-9542028-1-3

Cover illustration: "Complaint before the Prior"

Printed by Phoenix Colour plc

ACKNOWLEDGEMENTS

The boys who lived in this Reformatory have been present in my mind for over thirty years and I came to believe that there was no way of unlocking their stories so I am indebted to Albert Robinson of the Whitwick Historical Society who gave me the first set of keys from his own sources in the year 2000 and encouraged me to keep on searching. The doors were further opened in 2004 when Father John Paul Sanderson, Archivist at Mount St Bernard Abbey, gave me access to all the information about the Reformatory held in the archives and proved to be as enthusiastic as I was in having the story told. My thanks must also go to the Abbot and Community of the Abbey who have paid for the publication of this book; without that aid it must surely have remained just a manuscript. Unless otherwise indicated, Brother Martin Howarth patiently prepared all the photographs for me. Particular gratitude must be shown to the Superintendent Registrar of Births, Deaths and Marriages, County Hall, Leicester and her staff for their interest and willingness to search their old registers to find the names of those boys who died at the Reformatory and who will, thanks to their efforts at long last have some memorial of their lives in this beautiful place. Finally my heartfelt thanks to my husband, John, who has shared my interest and knew where all the paperwork was at any given time!

Maureen Havers 2006

CONTENTS

Introduction

Chapter 1 - The Catholic Background

Chapter 2 - The Legal Background

Chapter 3 - Abbot George Burder

Chapter 4 - Further Management

Chapter 5 - The Boys

Chapter 6 - Riots

Chapter 7 - Deaths

Conclusion

Appendix

Bibliography

Borough of Halifax

Order: in the

West Riding OF Yorkshire. TO WIT.

To the Keeper of the House of Correction at Wakefield, in the said Riding, and to all others whom it may concern.

WHEREAS *Edward Shanley* late of *Halifax* in the said Riding, labourer, was on the *Twenty fifth* day of *May* one thousand eight hundred and sixty *Six* committed by our warrant to the custody of you the said Keeper of the said House of Correction for the space of *one Calendar Month* and he is now in your custody therein; and by the conviction and warrant in that behalf it was directed pursuant to the Acts for the better care and reformation of youthful offenders, that the said *Edward Shanley* should be sent at the expiration of his said sentence, to some Reformatory School as we might thereafter name, order, and direct, there to be detained for the period of *Four* years, commencing from the *Twenty third day of June 1866*

AND WHEREAS the Managers of the *Mount St Bernard* Reformatory School near *Whitwick Leicestershire* are willing to receive the said *Edward Shanley* therein. Now therefore we the said Justices do order, and direct, pursuant to the Acts aforesaid, that the said *Edward Shanley* shall be sent, at the expiration of the said term of imprisonment to which he has been so sentenced, to the said *Mount St. Bernard* Reformatory School near *Whitwick Leicestershire* aforesaid, there to be detained for the period of *Four* years, commencing from the said *twenty third* day of *June 1866* And we do hereby command you the said Keeper to obey this our order and direction accordingly, and in the manner directed by Section Six of the Statute 19th and 20th Victoria, chapter 109: And for so doing this shall be your sufficient warrant.

GIVEN under our hands and seals this *Sixteenth* day of *June* in the year of our Lord one thousand eight hundred and sixty *Six* at *Halifax* in the said Riding.

George Holdsworth 〇

G. Buckston Brown 〇

I hereby certify that the above is a true copy of the Supplementary Order of the within-named *Edward Shanley* and also that *Edward Shanley* therein named, is identical with the person delivered with the said Order.

INTRODUCTION

Edward Shanley was the second son of Patrick and Betsy Shanley and lived with them at 16 Bridge Street Halifax. Edward was convicted in 1866 at Halifax Assizes of stealing two pairs of stockings to the value of two shillings and was sentenced to four weeks' imprisonment at Wakefield House of Correction and then to four years' detention at St. Mary's Agricultural Colony at Mount St Bernard Abbey in Leicestershire. He was ten years old.

By the time Edward arrived at Mount St Bernard he entered a system which had, to some extent, 'bedded down' and work routines and discipline were fairly well established; but had he been convicted even ten years earlier he would have been one of several hundred children in Britain who were at the forefront of a huge penal, political and social reform.

Justice cannot be done to the story of The Reformatory, as it was known, unless there is some attempt to unravel the complex strands of religion, monasticism and social reform prevalent in these middle years of the nineteenth century and the years of existence of the Colony at Mount St Bernard.

The first chapters of this book present a brief outline of those strands but it must be born in mind that each subject commands detailed scholarly works, so, where possible, those books which have proved accessible and informative are listed in the bibliography for anyone wishing to pursue the subject in greater depth.

THIS IS THE BOY WHO CHALKED UP "NO POPERY!"—AND THEN RAN AWAY!!

Chapter 1

THE CATHOLIC BACKGROUND

If it is at all possible to speak of the "religious ethos" of Britain in the early nineteenth century we would be talking of a land where the Established Church (of England) held authority in many matters of the daily lives of the people. In matters of belief, of marriage, of education, and, to some extent, social class, the Established Church was unquestioned but for both Catholic and Protestant the Church was rarely in the forefront of life - a part of the social scene which demanded little and was largely seen as the province of the middle classes. So the founding of a Roman Catholic monastery in England in 1835 where men would dedicate their entire lives to serving and praising God was indeed a work of faith and perseverance. Catholicism was the religion of a minority yet was seen as a potential threat not only to the established Protestant Church but also to the monarchy. There was confusion and misunderstanding about the spiritual allegiance of Catholics to the Pope whilst at the same time maintaining their temporal duty to country and Crown. The Catholic Emancipation Act of 1829 did little to clarify this. Under this Act, Catholics gained entitlement to vote, to enter universities and to become Members of Parliament, all of which could be regarded as empowering a group generally mistrusted. In the late 1830s the perceived stability of the Established Church was rocked by the group of young men known as the Oxford Theologians who brought into public debate their philosophical questions about the meaning of "the Church of Christ". (1) John Henry Newman was one of these men and his reception into the Catholic church in 1845 caused upheavals not only in the Catholic church but also the Established Church which then sought to distance itself from the "mystical heart" of religion and lean further towards a reasoned view of the Church. For the lay person with limited access to the arguments, the question presented itself not as a debate about the spiritual belief by which one lived and which defined the origins of the Church, but one of authority and allegiance.

For the Catholic Hierarchy during this time, England was regarded as a mission country and the work of its Vicars Apostolic was overseen by the Propaganda of Faith in Rome, but with the increasing number of Catholics during the 1840s, due mainly to the influx of Irish people fleeing the potato famine, there was a swelling of opinion that the Hierarchy, deposed for refusing to take the Oath of Allegiance during the reign of Elizabeth 1, should be re-instated. (2) Bishop Nicholas Wiseman was prominent in discussions about the issue and over a period of years various drafts of the proposals for Restoration were presented to the Propaganda, revised or rejected. Eventually the Hierarchy was restored on September 30 1850 and on October 3, in Rome, Bishop Wiseman was created Cardinal with the enormous task of heading the thirteen new Sees, a task upon which he embarked with jubilation and enthusiasm. These feelings were to be short-lived however, as he soon learned of the hostility of the English people. The Times reported the event with

> *"[Wiseman] …the new-fangled Archbishop of Westminster"* which *"signifies no more than if the Pope had been pleased to confer on the editor of The Tablet the rank and title of the Duke of Smithfield. But if this appointment be not intended as a clumsy joke, we confess that we can only regard it as one of the grossest acts of folly and impertinence which the Court of Rome has ventured to commit since the Crown and people of England threw off its yoke."*

Wiseman's Pastoral Address giving details of the Restoration which was read in all churches on Sunday 17 October added fuel to the flames by the incautious use of language such as

> *"we govern and shall continue to govern the counties of Middlesex, Hertford and Essex, as Ordinary thereof……"*

phrases which were taken up across the country with vociferous indignation. Wiseman wrote to the Prime Minister, Lord John Russell, expressing regret at the vehemence of the reporting of the press and reminded him that the government, in the person of Lord Minto, had been shown the proposals for Restoration some three years earlier and had received them without objection and Wiseman re-iterated *"I have no secular or temporal delegation whatever."* (3) But Russell was not to be appeased and in speeches and in writing condemned with forcible language the "Papal Aggression". By such means was the general public inflamed, perhaps unintentionally, but, the dispute coinciding with the early days of November, the ill-feeling erupted in a display of nationalism and anti-Catholicism. Effigies of the Pope were burned and the Guy Fawkes for the Loughborough bonfire on the fifth of November was substituted by an effigy of Wiseman.

Wiseman's response on his return to England was the pamphlet *"Appeal to the English People"* which addressed all the concerns in detail and by 20 November, some six weeks after his appointment caused such uproar, it was printed in full by most of the London newspapers and 30,000 actual copies were sold in three days.

Cardinal Nicholas Wiseman

Notes

1. Beck G A Rt Rev Ed *The English Catholics 1850-1950* Burns Oates 1950 p 7
2. *ibid* pps 42-46 give a detailed account of numbers and practice during this period.
3. *ibid* p 98

Chapter 2

THE LEGAL BACKGROUND (1)

The evolution of ideals and practice of punishment for children took over a century and it was the Victorians in the early nineteenth century who began to categorise children who broke the law as 'juvenile offenders' and to see that to deal with them in exactly the same manner as adult criminals was inhumane and frequently cruel. Prison reformers were appalled to see young people incarcerated in overcrowded gaols with hardened criminals, punished with the same severity and even occasionally, given the death penalty. In theory, children between the ages of 7 and 14 were held to be '*doli incapax*' but "proof" that they had acted with malice was often forthcoming and easily accepted by the dispensers of justice. No concessions were allowed to those over 14, the law and the execution of the law was inflexible and they were regarded as adults.

The motives for changing the system were varied but not least was a perception that crime was rising out of proportion to the increase in population and an apprehension that the rapidly growing numbers of young offenders would prove a threat to the established society, and there was a strong voice of opinion that these young people could not be reformed. Rev. Whitworth Russell who was Chaplain of Millbank House of Correction described young criminals as being

> "*trained to it from Infancy, adhering to it from Education and Circumstances, whose Connexions prevent the Possibility of Reformation, and whom no Punishment can deter; a Race "sui generis", different from the rest of Society, not only in Thoughts, Habits, and Manners, but even in Appearance; possessing moreover, a language exclusively their own* ". (2)

It seemed that one solution was to remove them physically from their environment, not into gaols where they might learn new and more sophisticated methods of crime, but into a completely new environment – the sea. In 1756 Sir John Fielding and James Hanway had founded the Marine society and collected public subscriptions to deal with petty offenders by sending them to sea, and the war with France was good enough reason for magistrates to use this avenue of "correction"; but life on board ship was little better than in gaol with the additional hazards of working on riggings, confinement below decks and the threat of enemy guns. Those young people thus sentenced were undoubtedly fortunate if they returned to their homes but later on, an even further exclusion was proposed. Captain Edward Pelham Brenton founded the "Society for the Suppressing of Juvenile Vagrants" in the early nineteenth century, which advocated a short period of placement at Hackney Wick (a Philanthropic establishment of the late eighteenth century for children in unfortunate circumstances) where they would be disciplined by constant employment and then shipped to the Cape Colony to apprenticeships previously arranged. It is not known how many boys were dealt with in this way but in 1839, accusations were levelled against Brenton of running a "kidnapper's Society" and the Society had ceased to exist by 1841. The idea of a new start in a new life was attractive to those who had to mete out punishment to young offenders and Australia was regarded as a land of opportunity as well as being a good distance away! Hardened criminals had long been transported to do the groundwork and it was thought that younger boys and men should now be sent to help in the second phase of developing a new colony. Many young people were sentenced to transportation in the decade between the 1820s and 1830s but, in practice, few got beyond the hulks moored in the Thames, at Chatham and at Portsmouth. These were disused ships of the line, the Bellerophon being the special frigate for juveniles from 1822 to 1842. The Bellerophon had been Nelson's flagship but its days of glory were over. During the twenty years of its existence as a hulk, 2,500 boys were committed to its decks, often confined to lower decks for 16 hours per day or subjected to hard labour. It was a case of "out of sight, out of mind" for the general public but the evidence of one Thomas Dexter to the Richmond Committee in 1835 attracted widespread concern. He had himself been imprisoned in Newgate and subsequently acted as a nurse at a juvenile convict hospital which treated boys from the Euryalis, another hulk. He was very familiar with the conditions afforded these boys and one bleak sentence of his testimony

"I would sooner a child of my own dead at my feet than see him sent to that place". (3)

spoke volumes of the horrors and depravity many boys encountered in the hulks. But even though the numbers committed to the hulks were large, the majority of young offenders across the country continued to be incarcerated in local prisons often for quite trivial offences, and despite the atrocious conditions, there was a strong public opinion that this was how it should be if it was to have a deterrent effect. The outcome of a period in gaol should be that the offender would vow never to return, but it was agreed that there should be a more systematic examination of the punishment and provision for those who committed crime and to begin to meet that aim, in 1835 Prison Inspectors for local prisons were appointed.

In 1838 the Government made its first intervention into the juvenile offender problem. The Parkhurst Act of that year established a new prison which was to be "stern in its aspect, and penal in its character" and only the more recalcitrant of young offenders would be dealt with there. Parkhurst continued in its original concept, punishment rather than reform, for nearly three decades . However, there was a growing public voice that young offenders should be given the chance to change their behaviour, that they would serve the country better as reformed citizens than convicted criminals and in 1847 a House of Lords Select Committee was appointed to seek the opinions of the dispensers of the law – the judges of the country. Their response did little to clarify the issue. Almost unanimously they were against transporting young people away from Britain but they were divided about the benefits of reformatories. Some thought that reformatories would not reduce the incidence of crime but actually encourage it, for in such institutions young people would be adequately nourished, trained and educated, all of which they lacked in their home circumstances. Prison, and the fear of incarceration were deemed the only ways of deterring young criminals. Juvenile Offenders Bills were introduced in Parliament in 1849 and 1850 by Richard Monkton Milnes who advocated increasingly severe punishments for persistent offenders in industrial schools or juvenile prisons with parents making payments to meet the cost of their keep but the idea that the State should establish and maintain institutions for juvenile offenders throughout the country was strongly opposed by the government.

The argument in favour of reformatories was by no means clear cut. There was disagreement about practically every aspect under discussion. Should minor or first time offences be dealt with by physical punishment only? A short, sharp prison sentence? Prison first then a period in a reformatory? At what age should children be sent to a reformatory? Should it be the responsibility of the State or philanthropists to provide the care? Who would meet the cost of care and training? The opinion that began to prevail was that which held that the counter-aspect of incarceration and punishment would be a system which would reform by kind but strict discipline, and which would include an education in morals, religion and basic life skills. This idea had substantial support but it was generally agreed that such a system would need to be administered by people focussed on the welfare of the child not merely employees of the state or charitable institution. Such a system was already in existence at Mettray in France and was rapidly gaining international renown for being successful in changing anti-social, petty criminal behaviour.

The Colonie d'Agriculture at Mettray near Tours had been founded in 1839 by Frederic-Auguste Du Metz and accommodated over 400 boys at a time in family type units of 40. Each family unit had at its head a master and two assistants and competition for excellence between the groups was encouraged. Such a breaking down of the whole number of inmates and a close personal knowledge of each boy by his house-master counteracted the "us and them" mentality and boys were encouraged to aim for monitor status, each monitor selected on a monthly basis by the boys themselves. Work and activities were strenuous and even on Sundays there was fire drill, military exercises and gymnastics in addition to church going. The boys were generally too tired at night to indulge in any plotting or misbehaviour and the consistent discipline and system of rewards was always overshadowed by the provisions of the French legal system. The Penal Code of 1810 stipulated a short, sharp prison term before transferring to Mettray and the inevitability of a return to prison if rules and regulations were not followed; but for those who toed the line and whose names were regularly recorded on the three monthly "table d'honneur" there was the promise of friendship and help for life from the Colony. This may not have seen much of an incentive during the boys' early days and months at Mettray but, having established a change of attitude and behaviour over a period of years, it must surely have been a beneficial and very positive type of after care which enabled the boys to turn to the Colonie for advice and encouragement instead of the criminal colleagues of their early years.

Many English visitors made their way to Mettray and there were frequent reports to committees praising the organisation and successes of the Colony though its ethos of a military regime was not seen as suiting the English nature. The concepts of segregation as punishment and manual work as reformation began to be clarified and there were notable exponents in the middle years of the nineteenth century. One whose name became widely recognised was Mary Carpenter whose compelling concern for children arose from a profound religious commitment to help the poor, and whose life was spent working far beyond the accepted role of a Victorian, charitable lady.

She held that no child was irredeemable and such was her conviction that she established a Ragged School in Bristol which quickly gained the highest praise from the Government Inspector for Schools but this system of education revealed its limitations to her as many children attended only intermittently and still found it impossible to escape from the pattern of minor criminal acts and subsequent gaol sentences. In 1851 Mary Carpenter's book *Reformatory Schools for the Perishing and Dangerous Classes and for the Prevention of Juvenile Delinquency* (4) was published. For the first time the subtle differences between 'poor' and 'delinquent' children were defined and the need for separate and differing provision for them urged upon the Government and the general public. The 'Perishing Classes' were those who lived in abject poverty and neglect, where health was severely endangered and who could, through the need for basic survival, fall into a life of crime, while the 'Dangerous Classes' were those for whom crime was already a way of life, who perhaps had family backgrounds of criminal activity and little 'religious or moral influence at home.' She further emphasised that there were differing degrees of crime; that some of it was primarily boyish high spirits and that boys from more prosperous families, though indulging in similar behaviour in their boarding schools, were hardly ever arraigned before the magistrates. The petty thieving practised by the poor was generally seen as

> "*that particular kind of delinquency which is most inconvenient and annoying to society at large, so one branded as a thief is usually regarded with as much repugnance and fear as if he were known to have a contagious disease.*" (5)

This perception had been most graphically stated by Rev. Whitworth Russell, Chaplain of Millbank (see earlier page) At the furthest end of the scale, Mary Carpenter admitted, were those whose crimes were so continual and consistent as to render them incurable by society. Mary Carpenter's vision received widespread public attention through her writings and appearances at meetings where she sought to influence those concerned about the level of crime in society and the young people who were the perpetrators. But she was not merely a theorist; she had had the experience of the Ragged School and had also, in 1852, instituted a Reformatory School at Kingswood in Bristol and in 1854 a Reformatory for girls and it was in these schools that she experienced the day to day difficulties of recruiting and motivating staff who shared her ideals as well as the practical and time consuming problems of changing the behaviour of the children, not by punishment which she saw as a negative influence on them, but by educating them into a way of life which would produce a '*habit of conformity to duty to God and to man.*' Mary's ideals had been formed in her early years by her father's ministry in the Unitarian Church and by his school which she attended as a pupil. Lant Carpenter's school was the antithesis of a Victorian school in that impersonal, authoritarian methods were replaced by a desire to build character through a caring, loving but disciplined family type structure. This early, very successful approach to dealing with children Mary saw repeated at Mettray and it was perhaps her unique vision and determination which enabled her to pull together the diverse strings of social, practical and - later - political concepts into a method which combined an element of punishment (the separation from family was punishment enough Mary believed) and reformation which was to last well into the twentieth century.

In 1854 the government passed the Reformatory Schools Bill which allowed for a certificate to be granted to reformatories established by private individuals. The funding for running costs and maintenance of the child would come mainly from the State with parental contributions of five shillings per week. The upper age limit for admission would be sixteen years of age and the young offender would first have to undergo a period of imprisonment of at least fourteen days. The enthusiasm for 'curing' the ills of juvenile delinquency was such that by 1856 twenty seven new reformatories had been opened and by 1860 48 certified reformatories were receiving over 100 committals a year and over 4000 young offenders were detained in them. (6)

NOTES

1. This Chapter relies heavily on *"A History of Criminal Law and its Administration from 1750. The Emergence of Policy in Victorian and Edwardian England"* Radzinowicz L. and Hood R. [Clarendon Press Oxford 1990.]
2. Miles W A Esq Second Report from the Select Committee of the House of Lords.......on Gaols and Houses of Correction vol 12 1835 quoted in *ibid* p 139
3. ibid p 143
4. Carpenter Mary *Reformatory Schools for the Children of the Perishing and Dangerous Classes and for Juvenile Offenders* C Gilpin 1851
5. ibid p 171
6. *"A History etc."* op cit p 180

Chapter 3

GEORGE BURDER (1)

In the early part of the nineteenth century when tolerance of 'public' Catholicism was just beginning to increase and the shadow of suspicion about Catholics receding, the foundation of the Cistercian Abbey of Mount St Bernard in 1835 was an act of faith on the part of those who promoted it and of the monks who brought the monastic life to Leicestershire. The Catholic Emancipation Act of 1829 had focussed public attention on the restrictions placed upon Catholics in Britain and there had been also some sympathy for the plight of French Catholic clergy who had fled to England to avoid suppression. The small group of monks who became the community of Mount St Bernard had autonomy in the running of their monastery and had to begin their initiative without the benefit of a Mother House or Father Immediate. The Abbot of Mount Melleray in Ireland exercised some supervision but neither abbey was represented at the General Chapter of the Cistercian Order, where principles and practice were monitored and agreed, until 1847. The lives of the monks consisted of 'Prayer and Work' evidenced by the construction of their first monastery, designed by William Railton, and the cultivation of the 'wilderness' of the area of Charnwood Forest in which they were situated. There is no question that the community was poor despite the gift of land for their monastery by Ambrose Phillipps de Lisle and a subsequent gift of £2000 from the Earl of Shrewsbury which enabled them to leave the original building and embark upon the larger Pugin design which remains today. These early years were ones of survival and hardship and it must be a reflection of the dedication, determination and perseverance of the early monks that they accomplished so much in a space of very few years whilst remaining faithful to the rigorous demands of the Cistercian Office.

Matins Two A.M.

During the next twenty years the monastery quietly settled into the landscape and the monks toiled to cultivate the rocky land around them and, gradually, the novelty of their way of life excited less interest from the local population. Suspicion about Catholicism raised its head again in 1850 with the Restoration of the Catholic Hierarchy and the hostility locally expressed in Loughborough by the burning of an effigy of Cardinal Wiseman in the bonfire celebrations on November 5th, has already been mentioned. Evidence of the level of concern at Mount St Bernard is shown in that Father Ignatius Sisk, a monk of the Abbey, was allowed to join in the attempt to quell the fears about the intentions of Roman Catholics by attending local Protestant Anti-Catholic Papal Aggression meetings but there is no record of his contribution to the debates.

In 1846, only eleven years after the foundation, George Burder had presented himself at the Guest House of the monastery having just been received into the Catholic Church. His reception had been a quiet affair. John Henry Newman, (later Cardinal Newman) himself a convert from the Anglican faith in 1845, wrote *"Burder and Formby are to be received next week but it had better remain quiet."* (2) Burder had been ordained into the Anglican ministry only four years previously and had served as Formby's curate at Ruardean in Gloucestershire. On June 5 1846 Burder entered the monastic community at Mount St Bernard under Abbot Bernard Palmer who had a reputation for being *"a simple, almost unlettered man but one who was known for his deep holiness and purity of life"* (3). Palmer had the awesome responsibility of being the first mitred abbot in England since the Reformation and it was he who had led the new community in growth and public recognition during those early years. Little is known of Burder's early years as a monk but it is recorded that in 1851 he was "Master of the Novices" and in 1852, when Sub-Prior, he gave two lectures on Monasticism at the Catholic Chapel in Brighton to so large a crowd *"that many could not obtain a seat – many of those being Protestants….."* and he was described as being

"a middle-aged man, rather stout, somewhat bald on the forehead, and about the ordinary height. He possesses a fine, full, clear voice, and a distinct enunciation." (4)

Abbot George Burder

Abbot Palmer died in 1852 and there seemed to be no obvious candidate in the community to succeed him. Mount St Bernard was by this time under the jurisdiction of La Grande Trappe in France whose Abbot was ex-officio the Vicar General of the Order and as it had been represented at the General Chapter since 1847 it can be assumed that the successes and difficulties of the House and its community were now more widely known outside the shores of England.

So it was that George Burder, a convert to Catholicism and a monk of only seven years was appointed Titular Prior of Mount St Bernard by Rome in 1852 and a year later was elected Abbot by the community. Despite his years in the Abbey, he had had little or no training as a novice of Cistercian life and it was said that what little formation he had been undergoing was curtailed by an illness during which he was granted the Cistercian habit for fear of his impending death. He did, however, recover. Burder went to Rome for the Abbatial Blessing on 21 December 1853 in the Church of St. Gregory and took his oath to Cardinal Barnabo, Prefect of the Propaganda of Faith instead of to the Vicar General of the Cistercian Order at La Trappe as was the more usual custom, and it could be asked if he already had some animosity towards an allegiance to a French House which was later to become explicit in his letters to Cardinal Wiseman.

We cannot know what part ambition played in Burder's thoughts. It must have been personally satisfying for him to have been elected Abbot after only seven years in the Church and in a monastic community in England which had a restored history of only twenty years. Those twenty years had been a period of extreme hard work on the part of the founding monks but by 1853 their life had moved from bare subsistence to one of a fairly regulated regime in buildings that were adequate for the number of monks in the community but with an income that provided little more than the necessities of life. So Burder's priorities did not need to be focussed on the survival of the monastery or keeping body and soul together but could be extended to make his personal mark in a world which, despite being cloistered and enclosed, attracted a good deal of secular attention. At home, Burder had begun building the imposing octagonal Chapter House but work soon ceased either because the funds were not sufficient to continue or because he became involved with other innovative ideas. Perhaps he had had grandiose plans to form new communities from Mount Saint Bernard for when the General Chapter of 1856 ordered that there should be no more new foundations, Burder reported to Wiseman by letter saying *"so here is an end to our proposed foundations in Scotland, Devon and Essex."* , {4} It may be that he felt constricted by the lack of autonomy of Cistercian life and the degree of control exercised by the French abbey; or it could have been that he simply could not lead the interior life of silent work and prayer demanded by the Cistercian constitutions, for in 1855 he had written to Cardinal Wiseman {2} that the Cistercian way of life was not in accordance with the will of God – an opinion he had expressed before being made Abbot. He felt that the Benedictine order was more suitable to the English personality, a view which was to become his main theme in the following years. Wiseman had replied to the letter and apparently suggested that Burder should write and consult on this with Mgr. Talbot in Rome who was deemed to have the ear of Pope Pius IX, but Burder perhaps saw this as a protracted approach and was keen to put his ideas before a higher authority and seek backing for them. In the next letter of 25 July 1855 {3} less than a week later, he had agreed that he would write to Monsignor Talbot but also he had asked Cardinal Wiseman to support his call to the Propaganda Fide in Rome for a Commission of Bishops to investigate regulations received from France and examine the matters he proposed and then report to Rome. He may have thought that the effect of such a Commission would be more immediate and carry more weight than letters written to a Monsignor, and Burder named the Bishops he would like for the Commission but, contrary to his acceptance of Wiseman's advice in the first paragraph of his letter, suggested that the Commission be requested without prior discussion with Monsignor Talbot. In this, Burder was exhibiting a trait which was to become more evident as time went on; he was very keen to get approval for his own ideas and suggestions and would seek to argue his case to the highest possible authority and selectively use the answers given to support his argument.

When Burder became Abbot it is probable that increasing the income of the monastery was still regarded as an important task and that many avenues of fund-raising were already being explored. In 1855, Dom Marie-Joseph Hercelin, the Abbot of La Grande Trappe made his Visitation to Mount St Bernard and suggested, perhaps as a result of financial discussions, that the Community could start a Reformatory for delinquent Roman Catholic boys as had been done two years previously at La Grande Trappe. It is easy to see that this could have seemed an attractive proposition because there was the possibility of it providing a solution to several difficulties; the payment of government grants could improve the Abbey's financial position; Roman Catholic children could be saved from losing their faith as they probably would do if incarcerated for long periods in state gaol houses or non-Catholic reformatories without the opportunity to practise their faith, and their life of crime could be changed to one of good, Catholic citizenship through the application of a loving but strict discipline in a place far removed from their criminal background.

Burder was enthusiastic and, without consulting the community, set about organising the project; a project which he hoped would bring national recognition and approval for the abbey and for monastic life in England and, perhaps, acclamation for himself in the religious and secular world. In 1855 Abbot Burder circulated a printed pamphlet outlining his proposal and asking for donations and subscriptions to be sent to the abbey. (5) In so doing he initiated events which would increase the demands on his time and responsibilities of his role to such an extent that he could realistically do justice to none. Now, in addition to being the Abbot of a community of fifty-five monks, responsible for their spiritual and physical welfare and the upkeep of the abbey, he also was obliged to adapt and extend the buildings of the original monastery to house up to 300 boys and to equip them with all the furnishings and equipment needed. He had shouldered a duty of physical, religious and reforming care of the recalcitrant boys who would be resident at St. Mary's Agricultural Colony and which would be supervised and inspected regularly by Government Inspectors. He was responsible for the young men he called "The Third Order" who took unspecified vows to him {32} and who would be engaged in the daily running of the Reformatory. In all the evidence that exists there is no suggestion that Burder initially delegated any of these tasks or sought help from any member of the community. In a comparatively short time it would appear that Burder had theoretically worked out all the implications of the venture and submitted it to the General Chapter of the Order which gave its approval in 1856.

Abbot Burder had wasted no time after the Abbot Visitor's suggestion in making a first written appeal regarding a Reformatory on 11 December 1855. He attended, and probably organised, a meeting in Birmingham of prominent Catholics and spoke eloquently about the plight of the boys and the duty of Catholics to save these children from eternal damnation. He reported the conversations with the Vicar General of La Grande Trappe in France who had first sown the seeds of the idea of a Reformatory in Britain in Burder's mind and why the Cistercians were so well suited to be the founders and managers of such an institution, dedicated as they were to the reformation of their own lives and characters especially through work and manual labour

> "the work being done by obedience, and offered up to God in the spirit of poverty and penance. There is, then, an affinity between the spirit of the Cistercian Order and the principle of a Reformatory". (6)

But to preserve and protect this offering of self - the fundamental aim of Cistercian monks - and to avoid too much involvement of the monastic community with the French Reformatory, the Vicar General at La Grande Trappe had had the foresight to establish a Third Order of Brothers who would have the main care of the children, whilst remaining themselves under the supervision of the Abbot and a Choir Father. Burder told the meeting that he had already appointed a Brother of the Third Order, a British man experienced at La Grande Trappe, to act as Superintendent of the proposed reformatory under his direction, (7) and that already there were others just waiting at the Abbey to take up their posts as well as candidates for teachers, artisans and farm labourers. He spoke of what he expected from the Third Order Brothers and what they could expect of the Cistercians

> "and thus the Abbot wishes that the Religious of the First, Second and Third Orders, should all have a common ground of union, by being all under the same Rule, more or less, according to their respective vocations and duties." (8)

Burder must have been confident of the approval both of this meeting and the General Chapter for he had already commenced on building work to enlarge the original monastery buildings to accommodate initially 50 boys but then revised to accommodate 100. The cost was £966.10s 3d. In addition there was to be a lodge built near to the Reformatory and more land to be rented - a total projected cost of not less than £4000. His appeal was well received for it was falling upon ears already familiar with the topic which had been predominant in the press for several years. Public spirited people had petitioned Parliament, and Memorials had been submitted with graphic details of the lives of young offenders and the prospects for them and for society if no action was taken. In an early Memorial of 1839, G.R. Smith had included the following statistics:

> ".... By returns made by the governor of the Westminster and Middlesex House of Correction, there had been committed during the year about to close (1838) 500 prisoners under 12 years of age (14 of whom were only seven years old,) who had been committed thither for theft or larceny. Very few of them had been sent from the sessions, being for the most part committed summarily by the magistrates, who had heard the detail of their several depradations (sic). It was further to be observed, that many of the transgressing children had been in prison three or four times during their short period of existence." (9)

From this meeting in Birmingham Burder raised a subscription list of prominent persons (10) and perhaps made the assumption that once an initial promise had been made it would be renewed on a regular basis. Some £4000 was either collected or promised in Birmingham and that, plus the allowances of seven shillings per week for each boy and other contributions to be made by the government (11) might have seemed a sufficient sum to ensure the viability of the venture. The Reformatory was to be the largest in England and it can only be imagined how Burder set about obtaining beds, mattresses, bedding, clothing etc in an age which relied only on personal contact or letter to conduct the enormous task of equipping such a large institution. People in the neighbourhood must have watched the inevitable increase in traffic with amazement as deliveries were made, but their reaction to the proposed Colony seems to have been unrecorded.

For the monastery, Burder's venture initiated a period of upheaval, turmoil and instability which ran counter to all the monks' aspirations and practices under the Rule of St Benedict. It can only be inferred from the various written documents which remain how much the rhythm of monastic life was disrupted but it does not take a great leap of imagination to "paint the picture" of the two years of great turbulence and agitation for all from the gaining of approval for the Reformatory from Rome until Burder was obliged to resign as Abbot. His energies were devoted almost entirely to the Reformatory and promoting it in the journals and papers of the day. Prior to the opening of the Reformatory and the committal of the first inmates, he had planned and printed a Rule Book (12) which set down in detail the daily routines and the way in which the boys would be introduced to a rural, monastic-style life. The number of staff he actually had initially is not clear, but in the Birmingham meeting he had spoken confidently about the experienced people waiting to do the work and in September 1856 he had written to Sir Robert Throckmorton that he *"had eleven brothers (who will be called Oblates of La Trappe) to take care of the boys"*, but there is later evidence that some of the monks were deputed to work in the reformatory [cf Father Lawrence about whom there is more in a later chapter] and Burder himself was not averse to taking on responsibility for the daily running. The Mount St Bernard archives has a copy of a letter in Mount Melleray archives of February 7 1858 to Cardinal Wiseman which asks that Abbot Burder be given "dispense from the Abbey for a short period, as we are in great need of his services." (13) It has 18 signatures, all prefixed by 'Brother' but whether these are Third Order Brothers or brothers of the community is not specified. The monks, of course, if asked, could not refuse to go to the Colony, being under obedience to their Abbot. Burder found himself unable to keep away from the Colony and had to be personally involved in everything related to it, delighting in every success and seeking to remedy its every problem. As before, he found it impossible to delegate. His euphoria in these early days of the Colony comes across in his letters to the press and, though not in his own hand, the following poem is most likely to be from his pen. It was printed as a leaflet entitled *"The Agricultural Colony (or Reformatory) at Mount St Bernard Abbey"* and sent by Burder to Cardinal Wiseman (14)

Song of a Juvenile Colonist

You ask me if I am happy here,
'Mong rocky hills so wild and drear,
And monks whose life is so austere,
St. Mary's child.
'Tis true my mother is away, nor are my sisters here at play,
But I shall see them one glad day,
St. Joseph's child.
Though lonely hills engird me round,
Both peace and plenty here are found,
With joyfulness I till the ground,
St. Bernard's child.
How can I else but happy be,
When holy monks take care of me,
Body and soul in charity,
The Abbot's child.
My sleep is sweet, my heart is glad,
How can I any more be sad,
No longer with companions bad,
Heaven's own child.

Abbot Burder's euphoria was short-lived and in the short space of time between 1856 and 1858 he became beleaguered on all sides facing problems in four crucial areas; the inseparable problems of the Third Order Brothers and the staffing of the Colony; the community of the abbey; finance; and, perhaps the greatest area of controversy, his belief that the English Cistercians should change their allegiance to the Italian Benedictines, a belief which he saw as a solution to all the other difficulties. The delinquent boys cannot really be regarded as 'problem' during these years for there is little in the way of negative reports about their presence or behaviour. The first problem arose from the earliest days of the Reformatory. Abbot Burder knew that the monastic community was itself unable to undertake the day to day running of the Reformatory and there was nothing in the Rule of St Benedict to allow them to do so. There were, thus, only two ways of recruiting staff; to advertise and employ lay people or to initiate a separate branch of the Cistercians as had been done in France. Mitigating against the former idea was that the wages required by lay people in addition to the burden of their keep would have a significant impact on the finances of the monastery and money was still in short supply. Lay staff would retain their independence and there might be a difficulty in attracting them to work in a local Catholic, monastic institution with memories of anti-Catholic feeling still strong. So the option of Third Order Brothers was crucial to the staffing of the Reformatory because those who accepted the role could be expected to be more sympathetic to the Cistercian Rule and life, they would be under the direct control of the Abbot living a type of monastic life as a branch of the community, therefore requiring only bed and board, and the 'Brothers' would have some degree of status in the Catholic world by being involved with this innovative venture, a status which might itself be an aid to recruiting further staff. The status of this 'Third Order' had little definition and the presence of a legitimate Third Order at the Reformatory has long been a source of controversy (15). It is not known how Burder introduced the proposal to his monks or whether he envisaged the Third Order as part of, or separate from, the monastic community of Mount St Bernard. His first mention of them states that young men

> *"have now an opportunity………of combining the many invaluable blessings of a contemplative and penitential Order, with a course of active benevolence….."* (16)

If Burder had indeed clarified his own thoughts on the status of the Third Order Brothers, this had not been conveyed to the rest of the community and the ambiguities soon led to dissension. In theory, the Third Order of an Order followed from the first order of Choir Professed – those men who had studied, taken vows, then usually accepted ordination as priests - the Second Order consisting of the Lay Brothers who also took vows but had no desire for ordination; and a Third Order would be those lay people who did not necessarily live in the community but aspired to adhere to monastic virtues of work and prayer in their own daily circumstances. Burder's Third Order was a great cause of upset to the monks and in Chapter the Choir Professed had complained that they could

> *"see that there is no stability about the Brothers of the Third Order – they are neither secular nor religious, without training, without novitiate, without vows."* {13}.

The Third Order Brothers themselves were also making their concerns felt and were *"dissatisfied and may leave and then we are thrown into the greatest perplexity."* {14} This crisis may have been averted for in October 1857, only one month after the previous letter, Burder wrote to Wiseman that the Brothers at the Colony had made their vows to him *"for one year, of poverty, chastity and obedience"* {32} There is no doubt that order both in the Colony and within the monastery was breaking down.

It is easy to dwell on Burder's involvement with the Colony to the extent of minimising the second area of difficulty which was in monastic terms the supremely important problem - his role as Abbot, "Father" of a monastic community which had every right to expect that he would be their spiritual and temporal leader and whose main focus would be on upholding and strengthening the vision of the founders of the community only twenty years earlier. This problem of leadership and authority became inextricably bound up with the third area of difficulty - concerns over finance, and far from conserving money Abbot Burder seemed to have been a slave to the adage "You have to spend to accumulate". The monks' reactions to Burder, the Reformatory and the boys can only be garnered but their indignation about his activities, and concern for the future of the monastery ring loud and clear from those written sources which remain. Burder is accused of "building up and pulling down" (17) and of unfinished grandiose tasks. The great octagonal Chapter House begun by Burder remained "unfinished and useless" (18) as he directed his resources to the Reformatory. A great tower had been built at the Reformatory serving no particular purpose. Discussions in Chapter had resulted in an agreement to stop all building at the Reformatory but Burder had disregarded this, continued building, and the debts incurred were increasing alarmingly. {18}

Financial problems were evident within a year of the Reformatory opening but no detailed accounts of income and expenditure were kept and debtors were pressing for bills to be paid. In September 1857 {19} a Loughborough bank loaned £1000 without security enabling some accounts to be settled. It must have been very difficult for Father Sisk to have his loyalties torn between his obedience to his elected abbot and the fate of his monastery, and there is a ring of desperation in his letter to Cardinal Wiseman where he accuses him of being biased against him and Mr. Phillipps and reminding Wiseman that he was not without experience and had in the past exercised leadership in the community as Superior. {23}He again wrote to Cardinal Wiseman {24}

> *"The Abbot is so changeable in his mind, and adapts his plans so suddenly, that we never know from one week to another, what he will do. His will is practically in all things the law of the House."*

As concern escalated about the Abbot's involvement with the Colony, the complaints became more specific. He was always up at the Colony; he was frequently absent from the Office; he canvassed approval for his ideas both in Chapter and individually with the monks, often asking the lay brothers to vote when they were canonically not entitled to. The monks had great fears about the Brothers of the Third Order who *"smirked and boasted that they would soon take over the whole monastery"*. Burder was accused of breaking confidentiality and discussing matters personal to individuals. It was also said that he had no time for the monks and that one could wait *"outside his office for an hour where he was busy with the papers, only to have him come out and walk right past without a word."* Money was an immense concern too and it was feared that the community faced bankruptcy but none of these worries was specifically addressed and Burder's solution for all of the problems was that the House should redefine its allegiance and become a Benedictine House for *"the English temperament is not at all suited to the Cistercian way of life.",* wrote Burder to Wiseman in several of his letters.

This lack of communication was a major difficulty for the monks who must have begun each day wondering what would unfold and, even, if he would be in the House. In June 1857

{8} Burder had left the Abbey, leaving a note to explain his going *"without formal goodbyes"* en route to Rome to the Congregation of Propaganda and reassuring the community that *"the House will not fall into ruin"* because of debts and insisting that he had founded the Reformatory, not of his own volition but *'under obedience'* to the Abbot General. On another occasion he left the abbey complaining that his state of health was such that he was near to breakdown and that he needed at least six months of quiet to allow him to recover. If Burder's mind was troubled, what of his monks as they tried to focus their thoughts on God through a rhythm of prayer and communal life constantly disrupted?

Burder was adamant that the root of all the problems they were experiencing was the unsuitability of the Cistercian way of life to the English temperament and he says that this was a view he had long held, even before being elected abbot and it was the arguments surrounding this fourth issue of concern which perhaps caused the most unhappiness to the community. Burder advocated that the house of Mount St Bernard should change its allegiance to the Reformed Benedictine Order under Abbot Cassarretto in Italy and that this more active way of serving God would lead to a happier community and one which could legitimately take charge of the day to day running of the Reformatory. This, Burder said, was not the only reason for the change. By becoming active Benedictines there would be more opportunities for personal sanctification, for the sanctification of the neighbours and *'for the conversion of our beloved but Protestant country.'* {9} The monks of Mount St Bernard were, almost unanimously, against this idea though some fluctuated and seemed to be influenced by the persuasion Burder exerted. This Cistercian community of just over 20 years standing cherished their history and their vows and held dear the fact that they were re-establishing a monastic way of life which had been predominant in Britain until the days of the Reformation. Burder had repeatedly presented his arguments about the Cistercian/Benedictine issue to the Choir Professed and to the Lay Brothers individually and also in Chapter, and had drawn up a petition to the Pope asking for his authority to bring about the change. Father Robert Smith's response to the petition is recorded as *"he would rather tear his heart out than sign"* {9} The staffing problem at the Colony must have been acute because Burder, in a letter to Wiseman later in August, suggests that the Pope could intervene and *"remove all scruples (about their vows) and every difficulty whether on the part of the community, Mr. Phillipps or the General Chapter"* {13} and that the General Council should give its approval to the dispensing of the Lay Brothers of their vows so that they could take over the entire running of the Colony. In this letter Burder takes a more personal stance against some of the Choir Professed, questioning their intelligence and vocation and suggesting that they should go to Australia and that the future prospects for the Abbey were bleak if we *"go on as we are now"*. New vocations to the monastic life did not seem to be forthcoming but the community accused Burder of re-directing potential novices to work in the Reformatory.

It serves no useful purpose today to speculate on Burder's motives for his actions or what it was about his character that drove him to be so blinkered about what he was doing and the consequences thereof, or how he could write to Cardinal Wiseman at great length refuting complaints about his personal behaviour but rarely seem to acknowledge that there might be another point of view and that he could be wrong. The daily events of the two years from 1856 to 1858 are revealed mainly in Burder's letters to Cardinal Wiseman which are in the monastery archives and the sheer bulk of this correspondence sketches a time-consuming activity which would preclude any other fraternal work.

It may also be unwise to draw conclusions about Burder's character or state of mind from his letters without the benefit of seeing those sent by Wiseman but a pattern does emerge from these letters of 1857 to 1858. Burder usually begins with thanks for Wiseman's response to his previous letter and a humble acceptance of the wisdom of Wiseman's words and his determination to follow the advice contained; but then what he has said initially is invariably qualified and he returns to the themes with which he is preoccupied. This may be that the community is against him with only a few exceptions; that the Colony needs a stability of personnel which cannot be provided by a Cistercian community; that the Cistercian Order is not suited to the English and the English temperament; there is often a veiled threat of the great public scandal which would be caused were the Colony to fail. These negative letters are interspersed, often only days apart, with glowing statements that the Colony is "good", the boys happy and reformed, the staff well-satisfied with their work. As the recipient of these letters Wiseman must have experienced confusion about the actual state of the Reformatory but even greater concern about the spiritual and temporal life of the monastic community.

There had been attempts locally, nationally and internationally to curb Burder's activities in the areas which were provoking confrontation. Ambrose Phillipps must have been the recipient of many complaints from the monks but seems, wisely, to have resisted specific interference with one or two exceptions. The General Council had placed a prohibition on further building or alterations at the Colony in order to try to conserve funds but the Reverend Sisk complained that Burder had ignored this ruling. {18} Similarly, in the heat of the controversies about joining the Benedictines when petitions were proposed and allies sought, Cardinal Wiseman had ordered that Burder was to keep silent on the subject, consulting or discussing with no-one nor seeking support from any influential persons outside the community. *"I have managed to do this"* said Burder but he was adept at using what had been said in a general context in the past as evidence and justification for his actions and for continuing his arguments. There are indications that Wiseman was becoming exasperated by all the problems at Mount Saint Bernard yet reluctant to give direct orders to Burder as to his conduct. He suggested that Burder alone should join the community at Casaretto if he thought that this was the correct place for his vocation but again Burder side-stepped the issue saying [I] *"will do nothing of my own judgement, for my own judgement is error, folly and sin."* {33} In this letter his language moves towards brinkmanship as he lists three "truths" which he will consider;
1. That the Trappists are not adapted to England and they cannot flourish;
2. If they did flourish, subjection to the French General Council would be a great evil;
3. The Observance of the Reformed Benedictines is exactly fitted for England;

and if, after consideration he concludes that all these are true, then he will - again displaying exceptional prevarication - ask Rome for direction as to his own conduct, but if Rome transfers his obedience to the Benedictines, then what, he asks, would become of Mount St Bernard? Cardinal Wiseman made another suggestion to Burder that he should resign as Abbot and take over the running of the Reformatory {53} but Burder was adamant that he would *"not take charge of the Colony if I am not Abbot and subject to a Superior at Mount St, Bernard."*

All the ripples and waves of complaint and discord of the first eighteen months of the Reformatory gathered force until in September 1857 there was a veritable storm. Cardinal Wiseman in his role of Apostolic Visitor visited the abbey with Dr. Roskell, Bishop of Nottingham, to see the situation in person and to try to establish some sort of order both in the Colony and the community, and at the conclusion of his visit he detailed his observations and complaints to Cardinal Barnabo, the Prefect of Propaganda. (19) To reduce Abbot Burder's contact with the Colony, Wiseman instructed that Father Robert Smith should take charge of the Colony with effect from 20 September and Burder, his options rapidly receding, initially gave his approval to this. Father Sisk, perhaps in desperation, had taken it on himself to leave the abbey and go to Paris and then on to the General Council where he had put his concerns before the Abbots. {41} The appearance of a simple, uninvited choir monk in this formal gathering of mitred abbots must have been almost without precedent. But Sisk's concern must have been recognised for on 28 September he again left the abbey and went to London where he met the Abbot of Melleray, France, and the Abbot of Mount Melleray, Ireland, and took them, not to the abbey but to Grace Dieu, the home of Ambrose Phillipps for discussion with him and Father Luke Levermore, monk of the abbey but acting as Parish Priest at Shepshed. This visit of the abbots was made on the instructions of the General Council, but when the party went to the monastery Burder most inhospitably turned them away by telling them that the orders of Cardinal Wiseman superseded those of the General Council, and that he felt that both of them were opposed in principle to the Colony and their visit had caused *"a very bad atmosphere in the house."* And yet on 29 September Burder's next letter {27} to Cardinal Wiseman swings incredibly to the positive with news that the *"Colony is doing well and twenty excellent Brothers……..are happy in their work."* Whatever the promises made to Cardinal Wiseman about his involvement with the Colony and despite the mounting evidence that there was now a huge concern about the situation, Burder was unable to detach himself from it or lessen his attempts to control it. After his initial approval of Father Smith's appointment to the Reformatory there was soon more challenge and conflict and Burder wrote to Wiseman complaining that Father Smith had gone to Nottingham without his permission saying that he was now answerable, not to the Abbot, but to Wiseman or the Bishop of Nottingham.

An important meeting in January 1858 at Nottingham saw Cardinal Wiseman, the Bishops of Birmingham, Northampton, Salford, Shrewsbury and Nottingham reviewing what was happening in the Reformatory, and discussing the causes and consequences. They concluded that the state of the Reformatory was most unsatisfactory, perhaps even critical because of

1. the absence of a competent resident superior
2. the absolute want of competent assistants

3. the absence of sufficient religious or even secular instruction
4. want of a proper confessor
5. want of discipline and cleanliness
6. the inexpedient union of the abbey and the reformatory accounts
7. financial difficulties
8. too large numbers
9. no proper classification of the boys
10. no feasible plan to remedy this state of affairs.(20)

Eventually Wiseman saw that it was essential to resolve all the issues concerning the community and the reformatory and asked the General Chapter meeting in France in 1858 to place Mount St Bernard and the Colony at the top of their agenda. The Chapter sought an even higher authority and asked that Pope Pius IX be consulted so that there could be no prevarication on Burder's part as to where instructions had come from. A visitation commissioned by the Pope took place in December of that year and Dom Francis Regis, the Procurator General of the Order in Rome, Cardinal Wiseman and Bishop Roskell of Nottingham spent two weeks at the monastery observing, with Dom Francis Regis alone questioning the monks. Burder was not in the monastery at this time having reluctantly agreed to remain in London while the visitation took place. Burder was asked to resign and he wrote to Cardinal Wiseman on 18 December a brief letter offering his resignation. (21) For the remainder of his life he stayed at various monasteries, did some parish work and also acted as Chaplain to country houses. Dom Bruno Fitzpatrick was asked to remain at Mount St. Bernard to allow the community to settle and to look for a successor to Burder. After some three months, Dom Bruno was convinced that Bartholomew Anderson *"would be the person, and no-one else"* [to be Superior] and his appointment was announced to the Community on the Feast of the Annunciation 1859 and Dom Bruno returned to Ireland, (22) but by now the affairs of the abbey and the reformatory were so entwined that they could not immediately be separated and it was nearly two years before the extent of the financial difficulties facing the monastery became clear. Tradesmen insisted on cash payments though some allowed credit (acceptances) on a fixed term but the new abbot wisely focussed his attention on restoring peace to the monastic community. A priority was to try to recoup finances to provide for day to day living and Brother John Jackson was given the task of writing to any who might prove sympathetic to the monastery's plight.

"January 25th 1860
To: J.A. Herbert Esq. Llanworth Court
My Dear Sir
We supplicate your charitable aid. Last year, after a painful investigation of our affairs, we found that we had been very deeply involved. It became imperative to make some arrangements with the principal creditors. Acceptances were unavoidably given them in settlement of their long standing accounts. Some to the amount of £1806 are yet remaining but almost weekly falling due. In addition our Tradesmen's heavy quarterly accounts demand an immediate provision.

We are obliged to borrow for prudent necessities. Earnestly
imploring your kind aid.
Believe me, My Dear Sir
Gratefully in Christ. John Jackson" (23)

Over the next two years Brother Jackson wrote some 200 letters in this vein, each of them phrased in a slightly different manner but with the same core message. The Abbey was in debt to the tune of £12,500; in twenty-first century terms he was trying to raise the sum of £1.5 million pounds.

NOTES

1. Numbers in parenthesis ( ) refer to the end-notes; for the sake of clarity and brevity in the text, numbers in parenthesis { } refer to the number allocated to the letter quoted and held in Mount St Bernard Abbey Archives.
2. Dessain Charles Stephen Ed *The Letters and Diairies of J H Newman* Vol xi Oct 1845 –Dec 1846 Thomas Nelson and Sons Ltd 1961 p 91
3. *Life of Bernard Palmer* Mount St Bernard Abbey Archives [hereafter MSBA Archives]
4. Brighton Herald September 1852 reprinted in *The Tablet* 18 September 1852 p 14
5. *The Midland Catholic Reformatory Abstract of the Proceedings at the Meeting Held at Birmingham December 11 1855* MSBA Archives
6. *ibid* p 3
7. *ibid* p 6
8. *ibid* p 6
9. Public Record Office Kew HO44/34
10. 52 names were recorded as having already given subscriptions.
11. The Minutes of the Committee of Council on Education (2 June 1856) provided funds for half the rent; one third of the annual cost of tools and raw materials for labour; grants towards the cost of books, maps and other apparatus and also to bear some of the cost of recruiting and training suitable persons to teach in the Reformatory. Undated letter Newspaper Cuttings Book MSBA Archives
12. *Rules and Statutes* undated MSBA Archives
13. Letter in Mount Melleray Archives copy in MSBA Archives
14. *Westminster Archives – Wiseman- Correspondence bearing upon the History of Mount St Bernard* December 1856 transcribed copy in MSBA Archives
15. Elliot B 'Mount St Bernard's Reformatory, Leicestershire, 1856-81' in *Recusant History* May 1979 and Tucker J L G 'Mount Saint Bernard Abbey Reformatory, 1856-81; A Correction' in *Recusant History* Vol 15 No 3 May 1980
16. *Abstract of Proceedings held at Birmingham etc. op cit*
17. Fitzpatrick Dom Bruno Visitation notes 12 9 1857 copy in MSBA Archives
18. Sisk Fr I letter to Mgr. Talbot 7 6 1858 Mount Melleray Archives copy in MSBA Archives
19. Elliot B 'Mount St Bernard's Reformatory or Agricultural Colony' in *The Adaptation of Change: Essays upon the History of 19th Century Leicestershire* Ed Daniel Williams Leicestershire Museums Publication No 18 1980 p 83
20. Arch. Prop. Fid. England T15 fol 130-1 Notes of Bishops' Meeting January 1858 quoted in Tucker J L G Mount St Bernard Reformatory 1856-81 A Correction *Recusant History* p 214 *op cit*
21. *Pictures of the Past* pp 39-40 MSBA Archives
22. *ibid* p 43
23. The Letter Book MSBA Archives

Chapter 4

FURTHER MANAGEMENT

It may be thought that after the experience of the Reformatory under Abbot Burder that the monks would be reluctant to see it continue. But that was not the case. There must have been discussions about the future, perhaps even heated ones, but there was a burden of obligation on the monks to the boys and to the catholic population but more importantly to the fact that the nation at large might revel in the downfall of a widely publicised catholic project. There would also be the major problem of finding alternative reformatory accommodation for the boys still at the Colony but, for the monks of Mount St Bernard Abbey the main bone of contention had been removed; there would be no more talk of affiliation with the Benedictines.

Father Bartholomew Anderson succeeded Burder and after a period as Titular Prior he was elected Abbot. By this time there were some 300 boys housed at the Colony and some Brothers, possibly the remaining 'Third Order Brothers', in charge of them. The Deputation of Commissioners which had obliged Abbot Burder to resign had asked Father Ignatius Sisk to act as Superintendent of the Reformatory and he experienced personally the enormous problems attendant in running a Reformatory. Father Sisk felt that it was imperative to not only have strong control over the Reformatory itself but also over the Third Order Brothers who were crucial to its staffing and to this end he attended the General Chapter of the Order in 1859 to ask the Abbots if there could be more definition about the 'vows' of the Brothers but for various reasons this was not possible and the request was refused and Father Sisk was left to manage a diminishing problem as no further 'Third Order Brothers' were appointed to the Reformatory. So the monastic community struggled on throughout 1859 gradually uncovering the extent of the other problems that lay ahead of them. The finances were in disarray and even without accurate calculations it was clear that both the abbey and the reformatory were greatly in debt.

If it was that the removal of the major cause of contention - the question of transfer of allegiance - had brought about a certain degree of peace to the monks it was not yet to be that their lives could return to focus on the monastic routine. The Reformatory and its management were still dominant issues and there was no alternative but to address them. The boys could not have been ignorant of the troubles of their supervisors and it is perhaps inevitable that their behaviour began to reflect the dissensions they saw around them and they responded to the inexperienced adults in charge of them in a predictable fashion. Anyone who has taken an interest in present day school activities will know that the discipline and control of a large body even of well-behaved children demands a high adult/pupil ratio and a consistent application of agreed procedures. For Father Sisk, plunged in at the deep end, it was a task of immense proportions.

At the Annual Inspection in 1860 Mr. Sidney Turner was accompanied by Father Henry Manning who was later to become Cardinal Archbishop of Westminster. What they saw cannot have impressed them and Father Manning stated his opinions quite clearly in a letter to Father Sisk on 13 December 1860. He thought that the monks should relinquish control of the Reformatory.

> "…whether it was prudent or not to attempt the direction of a Reformatory school at all, it is not prudent with the experience of the last five years to continue it."

> Also….."The Inspector Mr. Turner was with difficulty restrained last year from withdrawing the Certificate and his last words to me were, "If this were one of our Reformatories, I should act at once."
> "It seems to me, Reverend Father, that the Abbey would celebrate a Jubilee on the day that it could return to its own former state of freedom from the responsibility, anxiety, and danger of worse to come; and enter again without distraction upon the life for which it was founded in the beginning." (1)

There is only a bare outline of what took place over the next few months. Father Sisk left the Reformatory and within the next year the Colony was to have four further Superintendents. Father Aloysius Tatchell, then Prior of the community, took over from Father Sisk as Superintendent, (2) remaining there only until the autumn of 1861. The net for a Superintendent had been cast further afield and in October 1861 Canon Ward of the Clifton Diocese agreed to take on the role with the assistance of Father Hastings Thompson. It would seem that he was unable to stop the deterioration of the Colony and was asked to leave less than a year later when Abbot Anderson and the community at last decided that it was not in anyone's interests to continue with the Colony. Amidst all of the other troubles, six boys had died (3) at the Colony and there had been a disturbance which had resulted in four boys being taken before the magistrates. The community's relief at taking the decision was short lived, however, for Cardinal Wiseman pleaded that the Colony should be allowed to continue as there was no place for the increasing number of young Catholic troublemakers to go. Both of the other Catholic reformatories were full to capacity. So, the weight of the Reformatory continued to hang on the abbot's shoulders, and, perhaps reluctant to commit any more of his monks to the task they were physically or mentally unsuited for, Anderson asked the de la Salle Brothers (4) to take over. Negotiations with the Order appeared favourable and six Brothers were about to take up their positions at the Colony when the Government Inspectors challenged the advisability of an English institution being under the management of a French order. There was no choice but to abandon the idea.

The next approach was to a secular priest, Father Martin, who had been Chaplain to the Reformatory and had at least worked with and among the boys, but being a spiritual advisor was one thing and a Superintendent another and the difference in the roles was too much;

Father Martin was unable to cope and was dismissed at the end of 1862. (5)

The one to take up the mantle at this stage was Father Robert Smith whose health had been so badly affected by his last term as Superintendent and the situation he inherited could not have given him any cause for optimism. The boys' behaviour was increasingly unacceptable and even those recently discharged were falling back into a life of crime indicating that the training they had received was ineffective. In April 1863 there was a major incident when the boys reacted violently towards the staff and Father Robert had to send for the police to help him to put the boys into the cells. This event was widely reported in the press as was Father Robert's response when asked why he had stood by and not helped the police in the physical fight which ensued. *"The rev. gentleman said it was against the discipline of his order to fight."* To the modern ear the pathos of this statement evokes sympathy rather than condemnation.

It was obvious that the situation could not continue but the desperate need for places of reform and correction for delinquents meant that the Secretary of State, Sir George Grey, did not order an immediate closure. Instead he told Cardinal Wiseman that unless managers other than the monks were found for the reformatory its certificate would be withdrawn. They were to be given three months' grace. The prospect of nearly 200 boys returning to their dioceses branded with the tag 'uncontrollable even in a reformatory' prompted a response from the bishops. In May 1863 the Bishop of Nottingham called a meeting but few Bishops attended or sent representatives and the lack of enthusiasm for the continuation of the Reformatory seemed to indicate an opinion that it would be better for the catholic body to weather the storm of public scorn in the short term than suffer the responsibility of the Reformatory in the long term. Bishop Turner of the Salford Diocese (6) was the exception. For several reasons he felt that the reformatory must continue and immediately held a meeting in Salford to report the outcome of the Nottingham talks. Discussions had already been held there early in 1863 and a Reformatory Committee appointed to try to establish for themselves a reformatory in conjunction with the Liverpool Diocese but all the avenues explored had fallen through so when the problems of the continuation of the Colony were discussed, Bishop Turner proposed that the Salford Diocese take over the sole management of the Colony. The proposal was accepted on 29 May 1863 and the Reformatory Committee appointed four of its members to a Board of Management and the monks of Mount St. Bernard distanced themselves from the running of the Reformatory though Father Sisk continued to act as Chaplain.

Even from these very early stages it is apparent that the Salford managers had learned important lessons from what had been done before. What they wanted was clearly spelled out to the Cistercians and also to all those dioceses which had boys in the care of the Reformatory and who would be expected to pay their share of the running expenses. If such an agreement was not mutually agreed then that diocese would be asked to place their boys elsewhere. The monks asked for an annual rent of £200 for the buildings and 97 acres of land and sold livestock, tools and equipment to the Salford Diocese for £798 18s 5d giving a verbal assurance that the tenancy could continue on the same terms for as long as the reformatory was needed.

The Board of Management appointed Father Thomas Quick, newly ordained, as President and for him it was a return to Mount St Bernard as he had spent time there testing a monastic vocation in 1858 but had left to further his education. His short tenure as President saw another well-publicised disturbance at the Colony on 24 April 1864, a disturbance not denied but the reporting of which Thomas Quick alleged was grossly exaggerated. In a long letter to the Loughborough Monitor (7) subsequently reprinted in the Leicester Mercury on 6 June 1864 he refuted the claims in the article one by one and stated what efforts he had made to stem the trouble. The Editorial in the newspaper was sympathetic and agreed that

> "If such an incident had occurred in a Protestant Reformatory it would either have been passed over in silence as utterly insignificant, or at most made the subject of a paragraph in a news column;....."

But Father Quick was deemed too moderate and kind a person to exercise corrective discipline to unruly boys and was obliged to shoulder the responsibility for the outbreak and to resign his post. The regret with which this was received by the boys and staff is evidenced by a newspaper report of the presentation made to him by members of the staff when they gave him with a chalice to commemorate his time with them. His response to them is also printed and in it he says

> "I have loved the institution for years and I have had many moments of anxious toil within it. But I shall look back, I hope with consolation to that period as one of the most interesting portions of my life....." (8)

The next manager appointed by the Salford Board of Management was Thomas Carroll from Ireland and for eleven years he brought stability to the lives of the boys and under his management the farm was extended to about 500 acres with several new crafts being introduced, and at long last since an initial appeal by Burder in 1856, nautical instruction was begun and a ship's mast installed in the yard. The National Census of 1871 shows that a Michael White was employed specifically for the purpose of giving that instruction and he lived on the premises with his wife and three children. During the years of the Salford management, members of the Board visited assiduously, generally staying at least overnight so that a coherent picture could be built of how the Colony was being run. Their satisfaction and confidence can be judged by the fact that on more than one occasion Mr. Harper, his wife and daughters stayed overnight at the Colony while en route to Bavaria. (9)

While these years can perhaps be thought of as 'golden years' in terms of the boys' welfare, for the Board of Management there were on-going financial problems. From the start expenses had exceeded the income received through state grants and donations, (10) not in any profligate way but simply in the day to day running of the Reformatory. The Report of 1866 quoted a quarterly cost of £1000 to meet the basic needs of food, clothing and 'disposal' of the boys. Bishop Turner had made several appeals for financial support and stressed that not only was St. Mary's Agricultural Colony doing well but reformatories in general were beginning to show success in reforming delinquent children. He ordered that a collection be taken in the Salford Diocese to support the Reformatory and Canon Kershaw of the Board of Management wrote to The Tablet about the Colony and its needs and asked, rhetorically, whether the Reformatory should be allowed to collapse when in reality at least two more were needed to meet the Catholic demand. More appeals were made and collections taken and a Grand Bazaar was held in Manchester in October 1866 when £2,200 was raised enabling the Board of Management to pay off all of its debts. Father Sisk, still a monk of Mount St Bernard Abbey, was highly praised for his efforts in helping to organise this Bazaar and being present for the occasion.

The urgency of the need was certainly noted by the Liverpool Reformatory Committee which had been working towards establishing a Ship Reformatory but was hampered by a lack of funds. In its efforts to meet the estimated costs it was recalled that £2000 had been originally invested in the Mount St Bernard Reformatory and it was the members' thought that the financial problems of the Colony might result in it being sold. Should that be the case they argued, then all the resulting assets and contributions should be returned to the original donors. The Salford Board of Managers, in a meticulously argued pamphlet in 1868 demolished every one of Liverpool's points and demonstrated that since they had taken over the Reformatory their record keeping and accounting had been exemplary and the necessary facts and figures were at their finger tips. Concluding, they said that far from there being a debt of honour to Liverpool, that Diocese should pay the Board of Management some £700 for benefits received by boys of their area who had been maintained at the Reformatory during the Salford years. (11)

The Salford Board of Management then entered negotiations with the Cistercians about reducing the rent for the Colony and putting the tenure of it onto a firmer footing but the Cistercians refused all the proposals. The dispute escalated until it resulted in an Episcopal enquiry and in February 1872 the two sides met at the Abbey under the guidance of the Bishop of Nottingham. The situation dragged on and in May 1873 the Salford Committee sent their appeal to the Bishop of Beverly. Once again, Salford with the benefit of clear thinking professionals on their Board, spelled out in detail what they wanted and why they should have what they wanted. Their work at the Colony had resulted in great improvements to the land and extensions to the buildings and the community's argument that they objected to the existence of the Colony was not consistent with the opportunity they had had to close it on two previous occasions and they also had supported it in principle by attending the Manchester Bazaar to help with raising funds for it.

Whether there was a stalemate or the Cistercians capitulated is not clear but the Salford Committee continued to manage the colony. In 1873 Thomas Carroll resigned his post to become Land Agent for Ambrose Phillipps de Lisle but returned briefly, holding both posts when Mr. Kenning, who replaced him as Colony Superintendent, left after only a few weeks. The circumstances of Mr Kenning's departure are not known but it may have been that the boys were becoming much more unruly and even Thomas Carroll's previous successes in maintaining discipline did not manifest themselves in this time.

Bishop Turner had died in 1872 so had not lived to see the serious disturbances and the decline of an ideal he had so strongly supported. In 1875 the Salford Committee finalised their discussions with the Institute of Charity, (Rosminians) who had successfully managed the Market Weighton Reformatory for many years, to accept the management of St Mary's Agricultural Colony. Once again, the Salford Committee recorded every item to be agreed and at what value and at what cost and offered every assistance with the transfer that their tenure of some twelve years experience could give. They did not cover only the local aspects of the transfer but what should be expected of those dioceses that placed boys into the Colony. The arrangements were approved by the government and the agreement was signed on 30 June 1875.

Father Joseph Ryan became the new Superior and was only months into his office when the boys mutinied once again gaining unfavourable notoriety for the Colony and its managers. Another riot in 1878 was the final straw and the government insisted that a high wall be built around the Reformatory and the buildings improved but the cost was too great for the Rosminians and perhaps their will to succeed had taken too many severe blows to make further strenuous efforts. The government certificate was withdrawn from the Colony in 1881 with effect from 30 June. The nationwide publicity it had attracted over the years and particularly in the recent years meant that no other reformatory was willing to accept the 96 inmates remaining at the Colony and they were 'set free'. There is no definition of what 'set free' entailed and we do not know if the boys were released en masse in the locality of the reformatory or whether they were given the financial means to return to their homes.

Twenty five years of living in proximity with delinquent youngsters and constant haranguing about financial matters seemed to be at an end for the community of Mount St Bernard, and they sought ways to recoup some of their finances. The community seemed to feel that their best assets were in the buildings of the Reformatory which could be a good source of income and a copy letter (July 1882) exists in the monastery archives offering the site and buildings for rental and this letter provides particular detail about how extensive they were.

> To Capitalists, Hosiery, Smallware, Boot and Shoe Manufacturers and Corset Makers and others – To be let, on terms of yearly tenancy, or on a lease, the whole of the Convenient and substantial Buildings with their appurtenances and gardens, Nr. Mount St. Bernard Abbey, suitable with slight alterations, for adaptation to any of the above named trades, and until recently used as a Reformatory for juvenile criminals and situated about two miles from Coalville Station………..The Building, which is in good repair, Comprises rooms some of them the following measurements:-
> Two rooms 55 ft by 30 ft;
> Three ditto 56 ft by 21 ft;
> Two ditto 38 ft by 25 ft;
> Two ditto 94 ft by 25 ft;

Two ditto 72 ft by 30 ft;
One ditto 55 ft by 30 ft;
One ditto 30 ft by 20 ft;
One ditto 42 ft by 20 ft;
One ditto 63 ft by 20 ft;
A shed 63 ft by 24 ft;
A drying room 21 ft by 16 ft.
In addition to this there are upwards of rooms of smaller dimensions, (sic) the whole of which are capable of utilisation in manufacturing purposes, a portion being especially eligible as a residence for a manager. Gas is laid on to the premises from the Monastery close by and a supply may be had upon reasonable terms. An abundant supply also of both hard and soft water may be had at all times. A soft water tank containing 40,000 gallons is conveniently situated on the premises. A mill capable of being worked by steam power and an oven to take 50 stones of bread at once may with advantage be made use of. There are also convenient offices, workrooms, Bath, stabling for 16 horses, Piggeries, excellent granary with large and well stocked gardens, with or without 100 acres of capital arable and grass land. The possession of the whole may be had as one. An abundant supply of labour may be obtained from the immediate neighbourhood. The above buildings are also eligible as an asylum on a large scale, or for use by a laundry company, or they may be conveniently adapted to the purpose of an hospital or middle class school and a variety of other uses.

No evidence has been found that this letter cum advertisement was ever published but it may be an indication of the desperation felt by the community that even after their experiences with the delinquents they did not rule out the possibility of any young people being in close proximity to the Abbey. The scheme did not get off the ground and the monastic peace was short-lived. In 1884 boys committed to the Ship Reformatory, the Clarence, from the Liverpool diocese, in a spectacular mutiny, bound and gagged the staff and set fire to the ship which quickly sank in the Mersey. The Catholic authorities were faced with the problem of what to do with the boys and were saved from the option to 'set them free' by the government reluctantly giving them permission to re-open the buildings at Mount St. Bernard until another battleship could be allocated to them. The boys were housed there for about three months until they were relocated to another battleship, the Royal William, until it too was sunk in 1899 while the Bishop of Shrewsbury was aboard to administer the Sacrament of Confirmation.

The facts that remain about the management of the Reformatory tell the story of the upheavals, disasters and disappointments of the organisational side of the venture but in its day to day running there were men, and later a few women on the domestic side, who nurtured, disciplined and instructed the boys to show them a way of life completely different from what they had left. Leaving aside the inadequacies of management and discipline, there are only two negative reports about members of staff in all the years of the Reformatory's existence. Bernard Elliot records that in Abbot Burder's time three of the 'Third Order Brothers' were accused of sexual misconduct with the boys and subsequently dismissed (12) and Burder wrote to Wiseman on 29 December 1857 that he had had to dismiss one of the Colony Brothers for inciting some of the boys to riot, almost succeeding in his attempt. Most of the staff lived on the premises, the ten yearly census figures showing that the majority were Irish and that in the later years confidence on the part of the staff allowed them to bring wives and raise children thus making a real home in the Reformatory establishment, but these are the people who unfortunately live on merely in national official records. The story of the Reformatory is sadly diminished by the lack of the testimony of these men who were at the grass roots of the boys' lives and for only two or three members of the Reformatory staff are these statistics fleshed out a little more.

Thomas Carroll (1837-1918) has already been mentioned as a stabilising influence on the boys and he was Superintendent of the Colony from 1864 until 1873 and had been strongly recommended for the post by P.J. Murray, the Inspector of Reformatories in Ireland. Thomas Carroll was beginning his career in an already improving situation as noted by Sidney Turner in his report of 1865.

> *"The great improvement which I noted last year at Mount St. Bernard's has been amply sustained, the management and consequent progress being most satisfactory."* (13)

and by the 1870 Report not only was the management being praised but also Carroll; *"They are well seconded by the superintendent, Mr Thomas Carroll."* (14) Carroll was a firm disciplinarian but also a hard worker and remained at the Reformatory for nearly 10 years. Under his management the farm was extended by renting to some 500 acres and gained a reputation second to none in the district. Carroll encouraged a pride in work well done by allowing the boys to enter local agricultural fairs where it was not unusual for prizes to be won and the quality of shoes and tailored items made at the Reformatory resulted in sales throughout the Midlands. The number of boys committed to the Reformatory grew under his management until there were some 300 and nothing is known of his relationships with the monastery or the Salford Committee but whatever his personal feelings about the work he was doing, he was sufficiently tempted by an offer from Ambrose de Lisle to agree in 1873 to taking up a much less arduous post as the Land Agent of his estate. Despite the good reputation for the Reformatory built up by Mr. Carroll his successor as Superintendent, Mr. Kenning, could not cope with the demands of the role and resigned only a few weeks into the job. Mr. Carroll was asked to combine his role as Land Agent for de Lisle with part time supervision of the Reformatory until a new person could be appointed and this he did but the latter demanded a full time resident superintendent and by trying to manage both posts, the Reformatory suffered and discipline slipped. In 1874 thirty boys absconded and Carroll gave up the task. He eventually returned to Ireland in 1880 where he became Agricultural Superintendent of the Albert Institution, Glasnevin, Dublin where he was involved in research in controlling the potato blight which had had such a devastating effect on the Irish population during the 1840s. (15)

A rare picture of the relationship of the boys to the staff was given in "Household Words", a magazine to which Charles Dickens was a regular contributor, many of the articles attributed to him being written by journalists in his employ. One of these was reprinted in a "Guide to the Abbey of Mount St. Bernard" (16) and tells of the journalist's, Thomas Speight, visit to the monastery and Reformatory and it provides details of the boys and their surrounds which are not to be found elsewhere.

> *"After pulling a bell, we are admitted through a side door by one of the lads, an urchin of ten years old, who touches his cap at sight of us, and greets Father Lawrence with unequivocal delight……….A number of lads are engaged with brooms and pails of water in scouring the pavement; but everything is suspended in a moment, and a cheerful circle is formed round the Father, who has a smile and a word for each. After a little pleasant chat, and a few words of commendation here and there, we enter the building………Our entrance into the tailor's shop causes an instantaneous commotion. Discipline for a few minutes is flung to the wind, and Father Lawrence becomes the centre of a group of eager upturned faces. The Father puts various questions, chiefly on religious topics, which are replied to with more or less intelligence; and when he asks 'Which among you are sergeants?' the three red stripes are pointed out with pride by those who possess them. There is a lay brother in his dark habit, who appears to be superintending the youngsters. When he thinks it time to return to a state of order, he calls out 'Attention! Boys, to your places! Let us hear the clock tick!' The lads are back in their places, and we do hear the clock tick, almost as it seems before the brother has done speaking……..''*

Father Lawrence was obviously a favourite with the boys and probably one of those men whose heart was in the work he was doing and one of those *"who were seldom found for this work"*. More will be told about Father Lawrence in a later chapter.

Any research into the history of Coalville will inevitably reveal the name of Michael McCarthy and the evidence of his tireless work in the district. He was only 23 years of age when he first appears on the National Census of 1871 at the Reformatory and it may have been that he came to England with the express purpose of working there where there were at that time some 250 boys. It was McCarthy who initiated the building of the 'bath' or swimming pool and was instrumental in placing many of the boys in work on local farms and he had the reputation of always being one step ahead of the boys.

> *"There was never a lad born who could pull a fast one over Michael! He knew all the tricks.!"* And *"Over the whole establishment and routine, Michael McCarthy held undisputed sway, although tradesmen of the district – including a cobbler named Fox from Shepshed – were enlisted to supervise the industrial side of the curriculum."* (17)

Was it the pressure of the work or simple home-sickness that caused him on one occasion to ask the landlord of the nearby Forest Rock pub to lend him his fare to return home to Ireland? But fate intervened when he caught sight of the landlord's daughter, fell in love and subsequently married her. At some stage after their marriage he and Ursula (Hawthorn), his wife, took over the management of the pub and eventually raised a family of thirteen. One of Michael McCarthy's undertakings (after he had left the Reformatory) was to become a founder member of the Coalville Urban Council which was elected in 1894 and he continued to be elected to it for the next thirty-one years. The Coalville Times said of him in 1923

> *"Recent references in the council chamber to Mr. McCarthy show the high esteem in which he is held. Councillor James Smith described Mr. McCarthy as one of the best members who ever sat on the council...."* (18)

He died at Charnwood Towers (now Abbey Grange) and is still fondly talked about by his descendants who still live in the area.

Michael McCarthy

NOTES

1. Mount Saint Bernard Abbey Archives
2. National Census for 1861
3. See details in Chapter on Deaths
4. The de la Salle Brothers are a teaching Order founded in France by French priest Jean-Baptiste de la Salle (1651-1719). His focus was on the education of poor children and the Order continues today across the world.
5. 6th Report of the Inspectors   Elliot Bernard   ' Mount St Bernard Reformatory or Agricultural Colony'   in   *The Adaptation of Change: Essays upon the History of 19th Century Leicester and Leicestershire'* Ed   Daniel Williams   p 85
6. Lannon   Rev. David   'Bishop Turner, the Salford Diocese and Reformatory Provision' in *Recusant History* Vol 23   No   3   May 1997
7. Leicester Mercury 6 June 1864
8. Leicester Mercury undated copy
9. Reformatory Visitors' Book   7 August 1871   MSBA Archives
10. Lannon   Rev David   *'Bishop Turner ......'* op cit   p 400
11. For a detailed account of these arguments see ' *Bishop Turner, the Salford Diocese etc.'*
12. Elliott Bernard   Mount St Bernard's Reformatory Leicestershire   1856-81   in *Recusant History Vol 15 No 1 May 1979* p 17
13. Fourteenth Report of the Inspector of Reformatories P.P. 1871 XXVIII p 722 in Elliot Bernard   *'The Adaptations of Change.......* Op cit p 88
14. Seventeenth Report of the Inspector of Reformatories P.P. 1874 XXVIII p 590 *ibid* p 88
15. McKay Robert D.Sc ' *Pioneer Workers in the Field of Plant Pathology in Ireland; and a List of Papers on Plant Disease Investigations in Ireland Published Prior to 1940'* MSBA Archives undated copy
16. Jewitt and Cruikshank   *Guide to the Abbey of Mount St Bernard* Fourth Edition [Revised and undated]   MSBA Archives
17. Undated newspaper article MSBA Archives
18. Quoted in an undated article in The Irish Post   MSBA Archives

DIETARY TABLE.

	BREAKFAST.	DINNER.	SUPPER.
SUNDAY....	1 pint Boiled Milk and Bread, with Coffee, or Oatmeal Porridge occasionally—Bread ad libitum.	3 & 4 oz. Cooked Meat, with Potatoes — Bread ad libitum.	1 pint of Tea — Bread ad libitum.
MONDAY ..	Do.	Potatoe Hash, made with Meat—Bread ad libitum	1 pint of Boiled Milk and Bread, or Oatmeal Porridge (stirabout) or Coffee —Bread ad libitum
TUESDAY ..	Do.	2½ oz. & 3 oz. Cooked Meat, with Potatoes— Bread ad libitum.	Do.
WEDNESDAY	Do.	Potatoe Pie, or Hash, made with Meat.	Do.
THURSDAY..	Do.	Bacon, (2½ 3oz.,) and Cabbage — Bread ad libitum.	Do.
FRIDAY	Do.	Bread Puddings, & 1½oz. Cheese-Bread ad libitum.	Do.
SATURDAY..	Do,	Meat Soup, made with Peas, Rice, or Pearl Barley, and Vegetables —Bread ad libitum.	Do.

N.B.—The above Dietary is sometimes varied, soup, rice milk, or suet pudding with treacle, being substituted for the bacon and cabbage, or potatoe pie or hash; an occasional change being conducive to health.

Chapter 5

THE BOYS

It was against this background of conflict that boys came and went from the Colony and although there can be little chronology in their stories the fragments reported at the time provide glimpses which are almost cinematographic and furnish the twenty first century reader with a picture of the best, the worst, the bleakest and the most uplifting times that the boys experienced. For all of the various managers the main duty was for the welfare of the boys, their health and physical well-being, their training in practical and religious matters and, of course, for the reforming of their characters but there was also the legal requirement to keep records at all levels and however successfully this was done, few of these have survived. However, a contemporary with an interest in reformatories in general and the Colony in particular, collected newspaper cuttings into a scrapbook which survives in the Archives at Mount St. Bernard Abbey. Unfortunately the date and source of the articles were rarely noted but, where possible, the cuttings have been given an approximate date from the events related in them and used in this recounting of the life of the boys.

For all the boys committed to St Mary's Agricultural Colony, the journey from their inner city slum home, to court, to prison and thence to the wilderness of the Wastes of Whitwick must have been a profoundly un-nerving experience. For many of them it involved their first experience of transport; hours of travelling by train or horse and trap showed a world much greater and spacious than anything they had known and the sights and smells that assailed their noses would have added to that sense of alienation. And they were young, many of them not yet in their teens, and had been forced to leave mothers and fathers, siblings, and no matter how inadequate and impoverished their background there had been a constancy which had provided some sort of framework to their young lives. There were the few who were not so solitary and whose parental homes were deprived of not one but two young lads. The thirteen year old Shea twins from Surrey, William and John are listed on the 1871 National Census; David and William Driscoll (12 and 14 years respectively) from Tredegar in Monmouthshire were at the Reformatory in 1881 and the Bakey brothers from Bolton, Martin (14 years) and Stephen (13 years) were partners in crime in 1881. These boys could find some comfort with a familiar and trusted face but who would the young ones turn to? Ten year olds are recorded in 1881 – Thomas Lawley, Thomas Roache, James Toole and in 1861 Michael Dooley, Francis Burker, John Kehoe. John Casey also recorded in 1861 was only eight years old. What sort of hardened criminals were these? St Mary's Agricultural Colony, their new home for the foreseeable future was isolated, often bleak and subject to freezing winter winds, and the countryside extended as far as the eye could see, with hardly a human habitation in sight. This alone was enough to subdue the most recalcitrant child – for a time, at least!

Photograph from 'Charnwood Forest: A Changing Landscape'
courtesy of the Loughborough Naturalists' Club.
The Reformatory was situated in the trees at the bottom left of this picture.

The background of the boys was invariably one of extreme poverty. Many of them were of Irish origin, their families having immigrated to England during the Irish Potato Famine of 1848 and settled into the slum areas of north western towns such as Liverpool, Manchester and Oldham. Work was not readily available and educational provision for the children was virtually non-existent and it is not surprising that parents were apathetic and depressed and allowed their children to roam the streets and fend for themselves. Poverty and ill-health go hand in hand and many children came from chronically ill or one-parent families, or were orphaned and only superficially cared for by the extended family or neighbours. (1) Petty crime gave the children the opportunity of a small income, extra food, or at least, an excitement which gave a thrill to their mundane days but even though Mary Carpenter had been able to perceive that most of this juvenile crime was *"simple theft, more or less trivial"* (2) for the majority of Victorian society it was regarded as a serious and growing threat to the stability of the country. The various churches and denominations did their best to help the most impoverished, not only to improve their material quality of life but in order to encourage them back into the fold of worshippers that their souls might escape eternal damnation because of their neglect of their faith and unlawful practices. (3)

Apart from the material provision for the boys' life in the Reformatory, Burder had also worked out a comprehensive admission procedure to be followed as the boys arrived from the prisons. The policy was well thought out and not without merit and covered every aspect of receiving and keeping boys in the Reformatory's care. Burder's 'Rules and Statutes' ran to twelve chapters; every practical aspect had been thought of and this surviving document establishes a competence in Burder that is usually overlooked. However, it is unlikely that this complex and time consuming procedure could have been carried out with the level of staffing in the early years.

The convicted child, then, after his four weeks' imprisonment in his local jail and his journey under escort to the Reformatory would be greeted by a strange, tonsured person in flowing robes and the pattern of his life for the next few years explained to him. If he was fortunate enough to be the sole entrant on that occasion, he would have received a somewhat gentle introduction to the measured routine, sharply in contrast to his recent incarceration. But the numbers at the Reformatory grew rapidly as Magistrates were directed to commit Roman Catholic children to Roman Catholic establishments wherever possible and these were few on the ground, so the opportunity to be kept in isolation and *"frequently visited by the Superior and by the Brothers"* who would *"suggest to him wholesome considerations on his past life, and that on which he [was] about to enter"* (4) would be an ideal infrequently achieved. That this would have been the preferred option there is no doubt and it would certainly have helped to establish a rapport between staff and children, but for most it would have been "in at the deep end" with rules and discipline explained and administered as and when required.

A uniform of blue cotton tunic or jacket and a scotch grey cap was worn by all the boys and as a reward system was developed, red marks or stripes were added to these to indicate which of the three orders of merit had been achieved. As at Melleray in France, a "House" or "Family" system was established. (5) and in 1858 St Mary's had twenty-two boys; St. Patrick's 28; St. Peter's 30; St. John's 23; and St. Joseph's 32 and these families were each in a larger "Division" whose composition is unspecified. In Brother Stanislaus's letter to the Tablet in May 1858, he asks for an account of some "advice" to be included for the interest of readers. The advice was

> *"given publicly by one of our colony boys, Henry Gordon to his companions of St. Mary's Division this week. It is entirely his own composition.........No one suggested the idea to him....and his own behaviour and progress in knowledge and virtue since his coming to the colony has been very consoling."*

Detail from 'Laborare est Orare' by J Herbert 'Reformatory boys assisting with the harvest'.
© Tate, London 2006

Carved graffiti found on wooden plank in the monastery paint store 2004

Carved graffiti found on wooden plank in the monastery paint store 2004

Metal belt buckle found on the Abbey estate 2005

Henry Gordon was appealing to his companions *"to be good"*

> *"Last Sunday Brother Prefect held the chapter of our division, and only one hundred were called up for good conduct; he then said that he hoped more than that would be called up for good conduct next Sunday.........*
>
> *Now I wish to ask you if you think you could show the Brothers that more than a hundred can rise up, and, with a good conscience say 'I have been good last week?'.......... Look what our dear Rev. Father has done for us all; but look still more into the manner in which you should repay his paternal love, his affection, and the unbounded charity that dwells in his noble heart. He has loved you even as a mother, and more than a father.........Do you see where you are all; (sic) do you not think that this is a fit place to promise to observe the rules even to the last tittle; to show a good example in the ranks? If any of you has such a noble heart let him stand (at this all instantly stood up) forward and proclaim his intentions to all around, and let the Brothers see that for the future more than a hundred lads in St. Mary's division can say, "We are in the Section of Honour"*

The speech continues in a similar vein and while it is very probable that an older boy did appeal to his "family" in his own words, the lengthy, printed version is worthy of an orator, an educated person, even an abbot! But it does provide useful information about structures within the Colony and the way the press was used to elicit a sympathetic response to the venture as well as a subtle appeal to the public for money.

The most comprehensive description we have of the Reformatory is that of Walter White who visited in July 1859 and subsequently wrote in "All Round the Wrekin" in 1860.

> *.......*"*The factory-like edifice with adjacent workshops, and other buildings, yards, gardens and fields constitute the Reformatory, presenting a scene of order and industry alike satisfactory and praiseworthy. The boys about three hundred in number, from ten to sixteen years of age, besides secular and religious instruction, are allowed to choose any one of a variety of trades and you may see cloggers, smiths, tin-workers, painters, book-binders, shoe-makers, tailors, stocking weavers, carpenters and joiners, and other useful employments. A range of capability is observable; some prefer farm-work, and some have no faculty beyond mere labour, and are stone breakers and mortar-bearers. It reminded me of scenes of ancient pictures, to see a black-frocked lay-brother on a high scaffold superintending the roofing of one of the buildings. Go where you will you see a*

lay-brother or a secular in charge; which may be taken as a sign that the training of the boys is carried on as real earnest work; and if one may judge from a casual visit, the boys appreciate the endeavours maintained for their welfare. I saw none but contented or animated faces; and though some looked roguishly one at another, there was a general brightening up at the approach of Brother Stephen, and the worthy monk had ever a kind and gentle word to speak to the busy groups. Even the stone breakers plied their hammers as if engaged on piece-work at ten shillings the tone; (sic) and as for the smiths they clearly enjoyed smiting and shaping the stubborn metal to the music of the anvil. It would not be wise to forbid talking; but control of the unruly member is enjoined by example as well as precept. "He who keepeth his mouth and tongue, keepeth his soul from trouble" is written on the wall of the joiners' shop; and at the end, visible from every bench appear the solemn words "Oh Eternity, Eternity – All for Jesus."

The washhouse is well arranged, having plenty of space, and pipes for the conveyance of water led to a series of tubs and troughs in which a number of boys with bare legs were treading the soaked clothing. Whenever they look at the door they may read the invocation written thereon,
"St Stephen pray for us."

The gardens adjoin the enclosure and there I saw boys digging, hoeing and weeding amidst plentiful crops of cabbage and beans, and within sight of the cemetery set apart for the probationers. In the kitchen another party were shelling beans and helping the cook, free to enjoy the savoury smell of soup issuing from the coppers. Near the kitchen is the bakehouse, and above that a steam mill for the grinding of wheat.

The principal building is larger than appears from the front, having inner courts enclosed by the various offices, work-shops and apartments required for the lodging and training of the inmates. The bedrooms are clean and well ventilated; each boy has a separate bed, and in each bedroom sleeps the lay brother in charge, on a bed as little luxurious as all the rest. There is a good school-room, where you may see a music stand and hear at times the sound of drum, fife and trumpet, for martial music is not forbidden to any youthful learner who prefers it to soft and sentimental airs.

…..Yellow panes shining at the side of one of the courts indicate the chapel, a showy place compared with the

Abbey church. The altar was fitted up by one of the brethren who happened to be acquainted with the art of decoration and he has certainly made it attractive to the eye. Just within the entrance hang two coloured prints, impressive to the youthful imagination, one representing the deathbed of the good accompanied by the blessing of the Church and hovering angels, while in the other the wicked is shown lost to the Church, and a prey to spirit-forms which are not angelic;......"

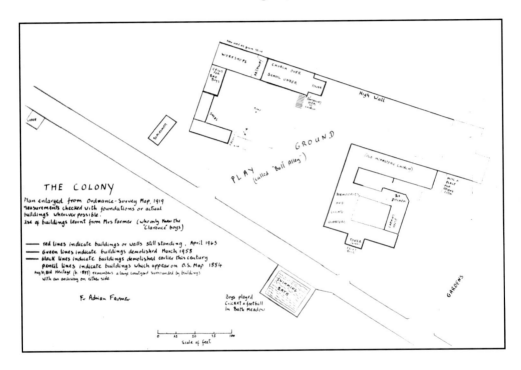

In all the reformatories of the nineteenth century it was regarded as essential that the children be kept occupied at every waking moment and the maxim "the devil makes work for idle hands" was a phrase which must have been in every supervisor's mind. The day was carefully structured so as to allow little time for personal contact or the opportunity for mischief making and to help enforce this Abbot Burder ruled that the boys keep the monastic silence for the greater part of the working day. (6) As the number of inhabitants rose rapidly this would have been very difficult to supervise and enforce and it is in the nature of most children to respond readily and positively to adults who take an interest in them, to chat to them and each other about the new way of life being experienced.

Chapter II.
DIVISION OF EXERCISES AND TIME.
SUMMER SEASON.

Working Days.	Sundays and Holidays.
Hours A.M.	Hours A.M.
5 Boys rise, wash, &c.	6 Boys rise, wash, &c.
5.30 Morning prayers in common.	6.30 Morning prayers in common.
5.45 Moral and intellectual training.	7 They assist at Mass.
6.30 Breakfast.	8 Breakfast.
6.50 Recreation.	8.30 Recreation.
7.15 Distribution of work.	10 Sunday report.
11.30 End of work.	11 Recreation.
11.45 Midday prayers.	11.45 Midday prayers.
12 *Angelus.* Dinner.	12 *Angelus.* Dinner.
P.M.	P.M.
12.30 Recreation.	12.30 Recreation.
1.30 Distribution of work.	2 Catechism.
5.30 End of work. Recreation.	3 Vespers. Recreation.
6 Supper.	6 Supper.
6.30 Recreation.	6.30 Recreation.
7.30 Night prayers. Singing.	7.30 Night prayers. Sacred singing.
8 Boys retire to rest.	8 Boys retire to rest.

The day began early for the boys – 5.15 a.m. in the Salford regime and there was morning prayers and school before work started at 8.30 and with such a wide range of ages to occupy, the division of labour must have been a logistical problem. Following the Cistercian tradition, Burder encouraged the boys to pray before starting their daily tasks – *"My Jesus, I do this for love of you!"* whether they were in the workrooms or out in the fields. Several workshops had been established and built by Burder; one was for clog making and in several of his letters to the press he requested orders from institutions to keep the boys busy (7) and to generate income for the Reformatory and the work of the cloggers is regularly listed in the Manual Occupation section of the annual reports. The Seminary at Oscott had declined to purchase clogs as the footwear was deemed not suitable for their students but an orphanage at Maryvale in Birmingham did buy clogs from the Colony for several years. The Reformatory was almost self-sufficient for its daily maintenance with small groups of boys employed in painting, bakers or as general 'house boys' but the main purpose of work was to equip the boys with skills which would enable them to make their own living when they left the Reformatory and even though these skills were in the main based on rural life, there was the added hope that the boys would not return to their previous inner city lives with all the attendant temptations for crime. The farm provided opportunities for learning about livestock care, for milking, for blacksmith work as well as for labour in the fields. In the time of the Salford administration about 38 acres of land had been reclaimed on the Charnwood Lodge Farm . (8) Boys were also set to stone picking or breaking, a never -ending job in the land around the abbey, and to building dry stone walls and digging ditches. Closer to home, the gardens were cultivated to provide produce for the table and there must have been great excitement and a sense of achievement when prizes were won at the Whitwick Produce Shows.

Newspapers of the period tell of many young people injured around machinery and there were, no doubt, accidents at the Reformatory but only two have been remembered in any detail. James McCarthy, No. 1298, aged 16 years, fell into machinery in the flour mill and his accident was reported in the Medical Report which formed part of the Annual Report of 1877. His injuries were extensive and there was fear for his life but he recovered after a long recuperation. Another accident involving machinery had a fatal outcome and is recorded in a later chapter.

Farm work is no easy option, but for those who take to it, it can generate a feeling of well-being and creativity and this is reflected in the bucolic painting of hay making at the monastery by John Rogers Herbert which shows in the distance a group of reformatory boys tossing hay stooks onto a trailer on a sunny late summer day. That the regime was beneficial to many of the boys there can be no doubt and as they progressed in self discipline and ability to work hard, so greater challenges and freedom were allowed. Laura de Lisle writes in her diaries that twenty reformatory boys, with supervision, helped in the garden at One Barrow after she moved in there and with Laura's reputation for caring for others, there was probably an excellent refreshment provided as a thank you. Some older boys were hired out to work on local farms where they earned the reputation of being better workers than many of the local youths. Some, the most highly trusted, were hired to farmers further afield and 'lived in' for four or five nights a week, returning to the Reformatory at weekends. Three lads from the joinery worked with William Worswick (9) and there was always the hope that they would be taken on in full employment when their sentence at the Reformatory had been served.

It was essential that all the work done was seen as useful rather than a token occupation of hands and minds and during the more settled periods of the Reformatory, projects were undertaken that were to have a lasting value to the local landscape and community and which are still in evidence today. The erection of dry stone walls has already been mentioned but this could have involved only a small number of boys as it is a solitary, skilled task and would need each boy to be paired with an adult. From an administrative perspective it was far more economical to have many lads working under the supervision of two or three adults and one major project undertaken was the creation or repair of what is still known as Colony Reservoir. The lake, now much silted and overgrown, is situated on land now owned by the Leicestershire and Rutland Conservation Trust but in the mid nineteenth century the land and grand house, Charnwood Lodge, was the home of a Captain Partridge. Frustratingly, little is known as to how the managers of the Reformatory came to be involved in this work but it is probable that negotiations took place to enable a constant supply of water to be made available to the Reformatory and the water from Colony Reservoir was then piped (with a natural down-hill flow) across the waste land above the Warrens, onto the Colony land where a large stone water tank had been constructed in Bath Meadow. The Heads of Proposals written by the Managers of the Salford Committee on the transfer of the Reformatory to the Institute of Charity contain the only information we have about the Colony Reservoir and the probable involvement of some of the boys with the work;

Colony Reservoir. Photograph courtesy of Norman Hall

> "The Committee laid out large sums in repairing a Reservoir and laying water pipes, hydrants etc. for the supply of both this farm (Charnwood Lodge Farm) and of the Reformatory."

The new managers (Institute of Charity) were asked to agree that

> "work [was] to continue on raising the embankment to render it thoroughly secure and that this work be completed within nine calendar months." (10)

Many of the masters and instructors lived in the locality and a story concerning boys leaving the confines of the Reformatory has survived through the generations of one family. Richard Fox (ancestor of Michael Wortley of Shepshed) was employed at the Reformatory and used to let one of the boys accompany him when he drove the horse and cart to Shepshed or Loughborough. It was Fox's custom to 'let the horse rest' at the Jolly Farmer's public house in Iveshead Road and leave the boy in attendance while he popped inside. On one occasion he came out of the inn after a brief respite and found the boy missing and the horse and cart unattended and feared that the lad had absconded and there would be some explaining to do. He looked around and spotted the boy in a ditch at the side of the road and demanded to know why he had left his post. The boy looked sheepish and held up a rat which he had succeeded in catching and killing. It appeared that there was a rat problem at the Reformatory and to try to alleviate it, the Brothers had offered the boys a 'reward' of a small sum of money for each rat's tail they could produce as proof of killing. The boy with Fox had heard a scuffling in the ditch and gone in search of the source with great success. Fox was touched by the boy's enterprise and honesty and allowed him to keep the tail and claim his reward without any detailing of where he had caught it.

Richard Fox
Photograph courtesy of
Michael Wortley

Stories such as this one come from the better days of the Reformatory but in the 'Letter Book' Brother John Jackson writes requesting information about oakum picking, where to obtain the untreated oakum and how to proceed with it at the cheapest cost to the monastery. It could perhaps be a way to produce another source of income, for money was sorely needed after the financial disasters of the Burder regime but also there was a need for the boys to be fully occupied indoors during the cold winter months when little work could be done in the fields. The work consisted of untwisting and unpicking old, tarred ropes so that the threads could be re-used and, as an occupation, it was heavy work, hard on the hands but it needed little skill and still less supervision or training. It was sometimes argued in the press that the boys of the Agricultural Colony were little more than a cheap labour force for the monks, for even though responsibility for the Reformatory had passed from Mount St. Bernard in 1863 it was still perceived as belonging to them.

It was the duty of all managers of reformatories, laid down by law, to educate the boys to a standard which would satisfy the government inspector on his annual visit. The majority of the boys received into the Colony had little formal education and of the fifty boys admitted in the year 1863-64, only 2 could read and write well, twenty six being totally illiterate. Similarly, of the fifty, twenty two were "quite ignorant of religion". (11) Burder had placed great emphasis on the religious education of his charges and perhaps used it as a vehicle for their literacy as they learned to read the hymns and psalms and catechism which were fundamental to their spiritual growth as young Catholics. The practical application of the Catholic faith meant receiving the Sacraments they had learned about – Penance, Holy Communion and Confirmation – and attendance at Mass on Sundays and Holy Days usually in the Chapel at the Reformatory.

The boys were given specific instruction in preparation for receiving the Sacraments of Penance and Holy Communion and, again, Burder could not resist the opportunity for a letter to the press. In a letter entitled "The Young Penitent Thief's First Communion" he writes

> "…….*If an **old** thief, as in all probability was the one our Lord so mercifully pardoned, if **he** was so speedily admitted into Paradise, why may not our young penitent thieves, so dear to the Sacred Heart of Jesus, why may they not be found worthy to be admitted also into Paradise; that is, to receive our Lord into their souls by Holy Communion, and that without an over-long preparation. There is something touchingly beautiful in the **first** communion of our young penitents. How they long for this great, this unspeakable privilege! One of them, a very sweet lad, was asked by a visitor if he was quite happy. "Yes", he replied "but the last three weeks have seemed very long to me". "Why has the time seemed so long to you, my child?" asked the stranger. The boy blushed, took off his cap, and said with a sweetness and simplicity that went to the stranger's heart, "Because,*

> *Sir, I am waiting these three weeks to receive the Body and Blood of Jesus Christ my Saviour." How dear is such piety and simplicity to the Sacred Heart!........."*

To our eyes the language is saccharin but prose in this style flourished in the Victorian press and was considered edifying to the reader, and it is perhaps indicative of the fact that many Catholics felt that they had to continually provide positive images of themselves to the public to prove that theirs was a spiritual 'empire' whose goal was to make good and law-abiding citizens out of poor material.

The practicalities of confining dozens or scores of young boys to the area around the reformatory have to be imagined and, inevitably, it wasn't long before they became familiar with the interior of the monastery and must have visited it unsupervised for Brother Ignatius wrote to Mgr. Talbot on 7 June 1858

> *"But soon the house was filled with them, even the Choir was not exempt, a place sacred in a particular manner to the Religious everywhere. Their low and unpleasant habits of life gave them [the monks] much to put up with in the way of trials."* (12)

The Monastic Choir

Further complaints came from Father James Luke Levermore, a monk of the abbey acting as priest at Shepshed who objected to the boys' activities in the church. He wrote a strongly worded letter to the Abbot on 21 August 1856 objecting to the boys singing 'with music' in the sanctuary. (13) There was a twenty-strong choir whose voices were *"soft and musical"* and they had been taught to sing, not only the Gregorian chant of the monks, but masses in several different parts to the accompaniment of an old harpsichord which Burder hoped that his readers could replace with a larger one. (14) The boys also had a band of sorts and Brother Ignatius complained further;

> *" Truly, the noise of the boys at their games, with their Drums, Fifes, sometimes when at a time when the Monks who rose at 2oC. are taking their meridian is some cause to complain of."(15)*

The rites and rituals of the Catholic church attracted interest and curiosity from the public and in the local villages of Shepshed and Whitwick there was a strong Catholic revival under the energetic ministry of Father Gentili, Chaplain to the de Lisle household, who drew large crowds whenever he preached and whose concern for his flock was legendary. Processions for the major feast days wound their way through the village streets and the boys in the Reformatory also had their own processions from the Colony buildings down to the new monastic church and around the monastery gardens. (16) Retreats – that withdrawing from daily life for a period of reflection, instruction and self-examination – were, and are, a particular way of Christian life and especially so of monastic life and as part of the Colony boys' religious formation, retreats were provided for them, at a level, it is to be hoped, in keeping with their experience and understanding. Burder reports graphically about one such:

> *"The first thing I determined to do for the spiritual good of the Colony was to have a Retreat given to our dear boys...............During the greatest part of the Retreat, the boys were assembled three times every day in the Colony chapel for instructions – instructions so plain, so fervent, so holy, that the boys listened to them with the greatest attention. The good Fathers (*Father Gastaldi and Father Vilas, Fathers of Charity from Rugby*) pointed out so vividly the nature and evils of mortal sin, the punishments of hell, the happiness of reconciliation with God by means of a good confession, the way to make a good confession and a good communion, and they painted sin in so vivid a manner, the arts, snares and cruelty of the devil, and the power and the love of the Blessed Virgin, that the boys were astonished and struck to the heart, and sometimes one might have heard, as the saying is, a pin drop, so breathless was their attention. The highest and holiest truths were brought **home** to them,*

> *and made level to their comprehension, by simple and beautiful and most striking stories and illustrations. They will never forget what they have heard in this Retreat."* (17)

It is perhaps not surprising that more evidence remains of the working lives of the boys than of their relaxation, and their timetable specifies only thirty minutes of Recreation during weekdays and with two hours being allowed on Sundays (18) so it can only be inferred that such a large number of (by now) healthy, energetic boys were, in fact, allowed the freedom to play beyond those times and within limited boundaries. "Cricket Field" adjacent to the Reformatory buildings and "Bath Meadow" in front of the Colony tower suggest activities to delight any youngster. Local knowledge insists that the boys swam in the water tank whether or not it was built for that purpose. At Mettray in France, a skeleton ship had been built complete with masts and rigging for the purpose of training the boys who wished to go to sea and a similar one was suggested for the Colony boys in 1858 (19) if the money could be found. Such an addition would certainly occupy bodies and minds but it was still being sought in 1864. (20) Money was found, however, to provide musical instruments and time was allocated for the boys to be instructed to a degree of competence which allowed them to appear in public.

> *"On Easter Monday and Easter Tuesday the boys had an excursion on foot, with their band of fifes and drums, to two of the neighbouring villages, where there had existed previously much anti-Catholic feeling. Many hundreds of the population – I may say, the entire village – in each case thronged the ways and the market place to see them. Our good and happy boys were the admiration of everyone. Our Protestant neighbours – the great bulk of the population – cheered them often and loudly as they paced along, with measured and military step, all so clean, so happy, and healthy, to the animating music of the fifes and drums........"*

Most of the 'excursions' of the boys were on foot and it must have been a sight to excite the local population to first hear their advance down the narrow lanes, then marching into view in a disciplined and orderly body. The villages of Shepshed and Whitwick are only a short distance away but an excursion to Loughborough, six miles, must have been a memorable day for those who took part.

"From the Loughborough Monitor June 3rd 1858
Treat to the Delinquents:
> *Loughborough was all in commotion on Tuesday in consequence of a visit by the juvenile delinquents from the Reformatory in the forest, comprising about 300, who were treated to a substantial dinner of old English fare, in a field of Mr. S. Ramsay's, Ward's End, which was kindly lent for*

> the occasion. Drays and wagons were decorated with evergreens by Mr. T. Hincks, and sent to the reformatory for the conveyance of the visitors, two of the former by means of scaffolds on top, were capable of holding 100 each. In coming down Iveshead Hill, one of them, owing to the great weight of the load, about five tons, was forced against a stone wall, but fortunately without doing any injury beyond a slight abrasion of one of the boy's legs. On arriving at Loughborough, they paraded the principal streets headed by their own drum and fife band, about 25 in number, including one large and four small drums, accompanied by the Rev. Father Abbot, and the brothers in charge with banners, after which they proceeded to the field assigned for their day's feasting and recreation. On each side of the entrance gates were large poles, with banners streaming from the tops, an archway surmounted with a sacrificial cross decorated with evergreens………Singing followed, and after the distribution of a small packet of sweetmeats to each boy kindly furnished by a lady, they proceeded on their way home at half-past three, in the same order in which they came, the band playing some lively airs as they passed along the streets……."

But these public appearances did not always go down too well with the public. In a sermon printed in the "Clerical Journal" and reprinted in the local press, the Rev. H. Fearon said

> "With singular lack of "sound wisdom and discretion", the authorities celebrate an annual holiday by parading the young criminals under their charge, dressed out in some kind of uniform different from a felon's dress, through the neighbouring towns, to be subsequently regaled with plum pudding and roast beef. As Loughborough was the scene of the last exhibition of this sort, the Rector of the Parish very properly considered it his duty to shew the inconsistency and bad effects of such extravagancies." (21)

If the boys were ever given to reflect on the comparison of their past and present lives, the contrast must have been of immense proportions. Here, where they were being 'punished' for breaking the law, they were adequately fed and clothed, their days regulated with work, prayer and instruction and, if they conformed to the discipline, there were experiences totally beyond their knowledge. At Christmas 1857 the boys were present at the celebration of Midnight Mass and Burder's account of it and our own experiences of the night-time rites certainly present a picture which would have stirred the hearts and minds of any group of young people. Abbot Burder had just described the death of Brother Lawrence and continued;

> *Great as was the shock of our dear Brother Lawrence's death, the Holy Mass commenced at the appointed hour, a little before twelve. ……but what deepened the interest of this holy function was the presence, in the secular part of the church, of a large number of the Colony Boys – that is, all who were in the section of Honour, more than 200. You may judge how great was my consolation to communicate 150 of the boys, some with the lighted candle in their hand, it being their **first communion**. Christmas here is a beautiful occasion for the first communion of the young, Jesus just being born. It was a most edifying sight. The boys gave each other the kiss of peace, as we do in the Order. From the altar it was communicated to them through the choir, Lay and Colony Brothers. A heavenly sight it was to see the dear boys making their loving inclination to one another, then giving and receiving the kiss of peace, then inclining to each other again, and coming up to the high altar in long procession, with their eyes modestly cast down, their hands raised, the palms closely joined, prepared in body and soul to receive their Infant-God . (22)*

On Christmas Day the boys were treated to a magic lantern show "with dissolving views" – cutting edge technology – with historical, moral and religious subjects being shown and for the best behaved, those in the Section of Honour

> *"……by invitation, have been to pay a visit to our esteemed founder and neighbour, Ambrose Lisle Phillipps Esq., at Grace Dieu Manor. Mr. Phillipps and a large party of guests expressed themselves extremely gratified with the order, appearances, and discipline of the boys. They sang several hymns, and the drum-and-fife band played their favourite tunes. Mr. Phillipps addressed them very kindly, and invited them again, and expressed a wish for them to go to Garendon on New Year's Day, when his Father would be delighted to see them. The boys cheered him right heartily, with "one more cheer"………..How different a life are they leading now to what they had two years ago!" (23)*

From the time of its inception the Reformatory was an object of curiosity and so indeed were the boys. Whether they were working in the fields, marching to functions in the neighbouring villages or merely milling around the estate, there would be people to stop and watch them, usually with friendly interest until the later years when discipline was weaker and the boys less willing to conform to the regulations. The more inquisitive paid a visit to the Reformatory complex, signing their names in the Visitors' Book or came in groups *"A great many holiday visitors"* and *"A great number of excursionists"* are recorded in June and July 1865. These, usually local people, may have been a small source of income and welcomed for that reason but there had to be an attempt at regulating the visits and the following appeared in the Loughborough Monitor on 26 April 1860;

"Mount St. Bernard Agricultural Colony

For the information of our readers and those who wish to visit the above, we subjoin the following regulations: "The Colony may be seen by visitors any hour between 11 and 4 o'clock, every day (Sundays excepted and Good Friday). Visitors are requested not to speak to any of the boys, or the Brothers in charge of them, but only to the person deputed to conduct them. No present, whether money or otherwise, is to be given to the boys, without the express permission of the Superior."

The Annual Report of 1864 lists in the Accounts of Income a sum of £1 11s 2½d as 'Contributions from Visitors' and also gives the amount of money given in Parish Collections in the Salford Diocese.

There were more well-known visitors whose names are written in the Visitors' Book; Monsieur De Metz who had founded one of the most successful Reformatories, Le Colonie d'Agriculture at Mettray in France visited The Colony on 7 May 1857, signing the Visitors' Book and adding the comment

"I have visited this Institution with a lively interest, and I leave it with a deep emotion, foreseeing all the good which will be realised hereafter by it, in having been able to convince myself of all the benefits which by it have been obtained already."
(Translated)

In 1865 there was a visit from Captain and Mrs. Algar of the 'Clarence' Reformatory Ship in Liverpool, an institution which was to gain national notoriety in later years and several Governors of Gaols came to see what sort of life the young people discharged from their care would receive. Most expressed themselves very satisfied with what they saw. The de Lisle family seemed to regard a visit to the Reformatory as essential for their more influential house guests, whether to see a social experiment in action or as an extension to their visit to the Monastery cannot be known. The Earl of Gainsborough and his three daughters made such a visit on 20 January 1870 as did Lord Clifford of Chudleigh and the Hon. Mrs. Clifford on 17 January 1871 and two years later on 18 November 1873 the book was signed by the Rt. Rev. Bishop of Nottingham, the Rt. Rev. Abbot of Mount St Bernard, the Rev. Father Prior of Mount St Bernard, the Rev. Chas. Dunne of St Joseph's Cottage and the Rt. Hon. W.J. Gladston M.P. who gave his address as Garendon. No record exists of what these visits entailed, whether they were escorted to all parts of the Reformatory, introduced to the boys and staff or if, indeed the staff were forewarned that visitors were expected and that the boys should be admonished to be on their best behaviour. The younger children may have been quite excited at the sight of 'ladies and gentlemen' within their premises but the thoughts and demeanour of the older, more hardened youths can well be imagined. One category of visitor seems to have gone unrecorded – that of parents, who, if they were financially able to make the journey, must have had very mixed emotions as they listened to the stories of reformatory life from their offspring.

However moving the nineteenth century newspaper accounts may be to the modern reader whose sympathies may tend to lie with the young people, a deeper response is evoked when new evidence comes to light especially if it had been thought that there was little more to learn. Such a thing happened when the monks of the present community were refurbishing a neglected part of the monastic building and when dismantling an old cupboard, came across a plank of wood heavily carved with names and crudely drawn pictures. The plank measures 10ft 5 inches and is $6\frac{1}{2}$ inches wide and bears names and numbers of boys who were probably in the Reformatory during its last years. One of the pictures illustrates a flogging with the recipient lashed to a cross shaped structure and it is a reminder that these children and young people were no strangers to such punishment either during their gaol sentence or at the Reformatory itself where physical punishment was used for extreme behaviour.

Whatever the boys' success in adapting to life in the Reformatory, learning a skill and developing self discipline, the public cry from the very early days of reformatories was "What happens next?" It was always a hope that the boys would not return to their home environment where a life of crime, probably escalating from the trivial crimes of their conviction to greater, more serious offences, would await them but there was little cohesive planning for after care. Burder may have thought no further than receiving the boys at the Colony and embarking on their period of 'reformation' but he was soon enmeshed in the public questioning about life after crime and punishment. His arguments initially focussed on minor issues – some boys were too old and too entrenched in their criminal ways to be sent to a reformatory and would inevitably continue their criminal activities; some were too young and even after five years confinement would still be in their early teens and too young to place in work. Perhaps, said Burder, some at the Colony would stay on at the end of their sentence and even become monks or, at least, Heads of Houses as at Mettray? Yet again he paints the rosy picture of what happens at the Colony – [we] *"keep a journal of every boy who leaves, correspond with those who have left us"* (24) This is in complete opposition to what Father Robert Smith had written to Cardinal Wiseman on 4 March 1858. (25)

> *"I told him that there twelve (sic) [left the Colony], and gave him the following account of them. Four to Manchester; one doing well in a situation I obtained for him in the Atlas Foundry; a second transported; - a third awaiting his trial in prison for theft; and a fourth dismissed by Daniel Lee Esq – for drunkenness etc. – Four to Liverpool; one ran away, and went to sea; a second, after practising much imposition returned, was*

> *employed at the Abbey, stole a watch, - sent away – now a soldier; a third enlisted whilst in a state of intoxication; a fourth after prowling about doing nothing, has been permitted to return, has been employed in the Abbey secular kitchen, turned out of it for bad behaviour, and is now supposed to be the thief that broke open the cupboard this morning – Two to Birmingham; no account of either. To Walsall one – enlisted for a soldier. To Halifax one, of whom no account has been given either by himself or others. Fourteen were sent yesterday with a brother to Nottingham to be enlisted ; and this by the persuasion of the Rev. Father Abbot. Thus of the twenty-six that have now left the Colony, we have one doing well, one a soldier, three unknown, three bad characters, - one doubtful, and seventeen soldiers – the Rev. Father boasted to me, that his was the best <u>Reformatory</u> in England – what a humiliation: what more powerful argument could the opponents of the reformatory system desire than this history of the boys that have left St. Mary's Colony?"*

Father Smith's frustration and despair cries out to be heard.

After care became an urgent consideration for all those interested in the Reformatory system and many suggestions were argued. There was a strong support for sending the young people to Canada – a solution which was rarely equated with transportation – and Burder advocated that someone should be sent out to Canada to locate people and places where young offenders could be employed and that perhaps the three Catholic reformatories in England could merge their provision for disposal with funding provided by the entire Hierarchy. (26) Others thought that the chances of employment were slim – once a thief, always a thief. (27) But whether or not jobs were found, it was felt that the reformatories had some obligation to keep in touch with the boys discharged and to encourage them to reciprocate. Mr. Fish, the Superintendent of the Castle Howard Reformatory, invited boys on leaving to return on Sundays for tea and regularly entertained past "pupils" but the boys committed to Castle Howard were more likely to have come from the surrounding districts thus finding it easier to visit. The catchment area for Roman Catholic reformatories was much wider and popping in for tea would not be an easy option. Personal contact with the boys was crucial and Liverpool Diocese made strong efforts through the St. Vincent de Paul Society and Rev. James Nugent who was well known for his tireless work among the Liverpool poor. (28)

As the years went on and experience was gained in managing the reformatory system, record keeping improved though it must be remembered that the science of statistics was in its infancy and comparisons between reformatories were not always reliable. The Report of the Committee of Management of the Colony in 1864, comprehensive and professional in every detail, tabulated the behaviour of the boys discharged during the previous year but the committee is warned about the comparisons made in the press:

> "The number [of boys] known to be doing well is a powerful
> argument in favour of the reformatory system, affording another
> ground of appeal for sympathy and assistance, and is upon the
> whole encouraging, although from the poverty of the great mass
> of the Catholics in England, and the paucity of Catholic
> Employers, we must always expect a greater per centage of
> relapses than the Protestants.
>
> We may also remark that the proportion of Catholic boys
> returned as unknown will always be greater than those classed
> under the same head in the reports of the Protestant
> Reformatories, from the fact that they are nearly all the children
> of persons in the habit of removing from place to place in search
> of employment, and often to considerable distances, so that they
> cannot be traced. It does not, however, follow that because they
> are returned as 'unknown', they have 'relapsed into crime'." (29)

INDIVIDUAL ACCOUNT—Continued.

No.	Date of Admission.	Offence and Previous History.	Date of Leaving.	Conduct of Boy since he left, and Present Condition.
7	Jan. 29, 1862	Larceny—First conviction.	April 9, 1864	Went to America with his parents; not since heard of.
8	May 21, 1861	Begging—First conviction.	May 10, 1864	This lad has not conducted himself well since he left.
9	Jan. 1, 1861	Attempt to Steal.—Had been convicted once before	May 14, 1864	Has been working steadily at his trade since his discharge.
10	Oct. 23, 1860	Larceny—Fourth conviction.	May 14, 1864	Going on well, working with his father a skilled artizan.
11	Dec. 22, 1859	Larceny—First conviction	May 24, 1864	Unknown.
12	Dec. 26, 1863	Larceny—Second conviction. Mother dead; has a very bad father	June 7, 1864	Re-convicted.
13	June 7, 1859	Larceny—First conviction.	June 9, 1864	Now in New Zealand doing very well. H paid for the passage thither of a companion in the reformatory.
14	Dec. 30, 1859	Attempt to Steal—First conviction.	June 11, 1864	Always a doubtful case. One of the committee obtained him twice excellent situations, but he misconducted himself, and has been re-convicted and sentenced t twelve months' imprisonment.
15	Jan. 1, 1861	Attempt to commit Felony. — Sent here on the third conviction This boy's mother is a brothel keeper.	July 11, 1864	Has a very bad mother; the lad went to sea t escape the dangers of his home. His con duct in the reformatory was very good

In its 1866 Report, the Committee spelt out the cost of 'disposal' of the boys:

> "The cost of disposal has been heavy, seven boys having
> emigrated, 17 been sent to sea, and 29 to employments found for
> them. The passage-money, outfits, and other expenses which are
> absolutely necessary, will always be considerable; and if any
> good is to be done to society in general, and to these boys in
> particular, a liberal outlay on this head must always be incurred.
> The expenditure in disposal has been £263 17s 2d in 1865-66, as
> against £96 2s 11½d in 1864-5." (30)

This Report also gives an individual account of the 133 boys leaving the Reformatory during 1864. Many went to sea, journeying to distant parts of the globe and four, who were discharged on 15 August 1864, went to America where they served in the Federal Army. All four were killed. Letters from the boys are included in this report all of which ask for their good wishes to be passed on to staff, often giving graphic accounts of the work they are doing.

> "Ship——————— January, 1866
> Sir, I write to inform you that I arrived safe in ———-after my first voyage to sea. I am very thankful to the Almighty God that has preserved me from so many dangers. One night it was blowing very hard, three more along with me were sent to stow the main top gallant sail, and I was out on the yard arm when the foot rope broke, and I had to hang down by two small points till the other three men came out and saved me, thank God. We had some awful weather coming home; it blew so hard that the Captain thought we would go down every minute. We were 98 days going out to St. John's, New Brunswick. I send my respects to Mr. Wisely, and also to Mr. Crute and his wife if they are there. Write to Father John O'Brien and tell him that I have arrived safe, and I am very thankful to him for his kindness."(31)

The Reverend Sidney Turner had proposed a 'ticket of leave' for lads whose conduct had improved sufficiently and who were not yet candidates for total discharge. This was a type of probation allowing them to return home on condition of good behaviour and no criminal activity, but it was a system difficult to monitor and prohibitively expensive to organise fully. In addition, public opinion was much against it as it was seen as being soft on the criminal and failing to uphold the sentence of the law. Where this was tried, the boys were told in advance that they were being considered for such discharge and they usually responded with excellent behaviour to achieve the goal of leaving. If this was subsequently refused, a return to bad behaviour was almost inevitable, as was thought to have been one of the causes of the riot in 1863.

'Disposal' or 'Discharge' of the boys remained a continual problem and perhaps not always carried out in their best interests. As the number of young offenders committed increased, the space in the reformatories was at a premium and there may have been an unspoken policy not only to move on the good, the well-behaved, but those of a more troublesome nature. The army was eager for recruits and the 'carrot' of wages, travel to foreign countries and a discipline they had already mastered was eagerly grasped by the lads keen to escape the confines of the reformatories. On 3 December 1870 Father Sisk wrote to the Duke of Portland about the difficulties of making sure the boys had some prospects for the future after their discharge from the Reformatory. He said that more than 1100 boys had passed through the Reformatory since it had opened and that it was his belief that a future in Canada was in their best interests. But the cost was prohibitive and he detailed the expense of settling a boy in a new country – some £600. (32)

The efforts of individuals, church societies and management committees to secure a bright future for the boys who had spent several years in the reformatory institutions demonstrated a commitment to the boys probably beyond anything of their previous experience and there must have been many who were able to make a new life for themselves by reason of this help. For others, at least in the short term, their only ambition was to escape the confines and discipline of the reformatory and they determined to use any means to achieve that end.

NOTES

1. The Annual Report of 1864 states that of 50 boys admitted that year 2 were orphans and 21 from families where one parent was dead. MSBA Archives
2. Radzinowicz L and Hood R *The Emergence of Penal Policy in Victorian and Edwardian England* (Clarendon Press 1990) p 164
3. For an account of Father James Nugent's life see Furnival John *Children of the Second Spring Father James Nugent and the Work of Child Care in Liverpool* Leominster Gracewing 2005
4. *Rules and Statutes* MSBA Archives
5. Letter from Bro Stanislaus to *The Tablet* 7 5 1858 Press Cuttings Book MSBA Archives
6. Rule Book MSBA Archives
7. *"The boys can make good Lancashire clogs and we should be glad to have orders for them. "* Burder letter Press Cuttings Book 22 4 1857 MSBA Archives
8. Salford Diocese Heads of Proposals 30 6 1875 MSBA Archives
9. *Annual Report of the Reformatory School Mount St Bernard's near Coalville, Leicestershire 1866* "Three of our joiner lads worked in the carpenter's shop at the collieries of W. Worswick, Esq., and, through the kind co-operation of his manager, one of them saved sufficient money to purchase tools, and pay the cost of the emigration to Novia Scotia of himself and a companion from the Reformatory. p 10 British Library RB 23 a.19416
10. Heads of Proposals op cit 30 6 1875
11. *Annual Report etc* 10 12 1864 p15
12. Letter in Mount Melleray Archives Copy in MSBA Archives
13. Letter in MSBA Archives
14. Press cuttings Book 22 4 1857 MSBA Archives
15. *ibid* 19 5 1857
16. *ibid* 19.5.1857
17. *ibid* undated
18. *Annual Report etc.....1864* p17
19. Burder letter to *The Tablet* 7 5 1858 Press Cuttings Book MSBA Archives
20. *Annual Report etc ....1864* op cit p11
21. Press Cuttings Book MSBA Archives
22. Burder letter to *The Weekly Register* 27 12 1857 Press Cuttings Book MSBA Archives
23. *ibid.*
24. Press Cuttings Book 27 4 1858 MSBA Archives
25. MSBA Archives
26. Press Cuttings Book Easter Sunday 1858
27. Press Cuttings Book 11 5 1858
28. *Annual Report etc.....1866* op cit p 7
29. *Annual Report etc... 1864* op cit p 12
30. *Annual Report etc....1866* op cit p 7
31. *Annual Report etc... 1866* op cit p 15
32. MSBA Archives

The Colony, Mount St Bernard Abbey

Chapter 6

RIOTS

In the thirty years of the Reformatory's existence in the vicinity of Mount St Bernard it is perhaps a wry comment on human nature that so little is remembered of the positive aspects of the regime but everyone knows something about 'The Riots' which took place in the 1860s and 1870s. Accounts of these disturbances not only filled the local press but were reported in the national newspapers and even brought up in Parliament. Was it perhaps a matter of the 'worst case scenario' realised – hordes of youths, known and convicted criminals defying and defeating the control of their gaolers and rampaging around the once peaceful countryside; doors of isolated cottages in normal circumstances never secured, now locked, barred and bolted as the news of a break-out spread rapidly by word of mouth? Or was it as described by 'Lavengro' in the Coalville Times in April 1970

> *"The discipline inside the reformatory was rigid enough, but when stories began to circulate regarding escapes they were accompanied by allegations of cruelty against the lads. Such rumours may or may not have been founded on fact, but local public sympathies were invariably with the lads and there were times when assistance was actually given to the escapees."*

Burder acknowledged that [we]

> *"have had, it is true, runaways, how could it be otherwise? but these have either come back of their own accord, or have been brought back, apparently not at all displeased at their capture."* (1)

He insists that such boys were punished with "justice and mercy" before the assembled Colony. It was perhaps these boys who received the sympathy and collaboration of the locals.

Initial inspection reports on the Colony were quite favourable but the boys' behaviour deteriorated during 1858 as Burder struggled to keep control over the Reformatory in the face of ever-increasing problems there and the consequent disruption to community life at the monastery and by the time the Reformatory came under the management of the Salford Diocese, there was a hard core of boys whose behaviour was such that other reformatories had refused to admit them or agree to their transfer on the take-over. The first serious trouble came in April of 1863 when Father Robert Smith was yet again Superior of the Colony and a twenty-first century re-telling of the events cannot hope to evoke the picture painted so graphically by a local reporter. His first paragraph gives a brief history of the monastery and the self-discipline of the monks.

"Source: Leicester Journal
Date Friday, April 17th 1863

CONSPIRACY & MUTINY
At
St. Bernard's Reformatory

(From our Special Reporter)

...............the criminals, however, fail to appreciate the precept and example which they have from their Roman Catholic tutors, and have rebelled. The insurrectionary movement being preconceived, artfully planned, and determinedly executed, has been attended with disastrous and nearly fatal results. In May, 1858 there was an outbreak in this establishment, which ended in four of the prominent parties being brought to justice; now there has been a recurrence, prosecuted with redoubled energy.

The diet and regulations of the Reformatory are good, and we should imagine could give no cause of complaint. Various rumours having got abroad with regard to the conduct of the house, we ourselves have taken the pains to make enquiry and personal inspection as to these matters, in order that we may be in a position to furnish our readers with authoritative information on the subject. The Reformatory, we may observe, stands upon almost 100 acres of ground, and resembles to outward appearance a large farmstead. Suitable buildings are erected for industrial purposes. There are gardeners and farm labourers outside the premises, and inside you may see at work the blacksmith, the tailor, the carpenter, the shoemaker, the baker and the cook. There is a school well furnished and comfortable looking, an intelligent master, and every provision for instruction. Believing the old proverb that "all work and no play makes Jack a dull boy", ample room is afforded for recreational purposes. Open and covered playgrounds are there, and at certain periods during the day, the boys are allowed to lay down their various implements of their calling, and refresh themselves by engaging in popular sports and pastimes. The orders of the day are somewhat as follows:- From 6a.m. to 7.30 at school; from 7.30 until 8.15, breakfast; from 8.15 until 11.45 employment at their various trades; from 11.45 until 12, general orders as to dinner; from 12 to 1, dinner and play; from 1 until 4.45 work; from 4.45 to 6, tea and recreation; from 6 until 7.30 school. The boys attend church three times on Sunday and once during the week. The present superior is Father Roberts; the schoolmaster, Mr. Jas. Collins; the procurator, Mr. Murphy; the secretary, Mr. Edwards; overlooker of work, Mr. Tomkins; discipline master, Mr. Brean and a constable named Kelly. The cooking and washing and other work necessary for the conduct of the house is done by the boys, the number at present confined there being about 180. Their terms of imprisonment vary from three to five years, and the towns from which they come are principally Birmingham, Manchester and Liverpool, their associates having been rogues and vagabonds.

It seems to have been imagined by many of the criminals in this Reformatory that they would be dealt with somewhat after the fashion of ticket of leave convicts, that is, having been sentenced to a term of five years' imprisonment they would be liberated after patient endurance for a year or two. Not finding any such prospect before them of being again permitted to enjoy the sweets of liberty, and being tired of the durance vile of the Reformatory, a number contemplated making their escape. They were determined to do this by foul means if their more subtle contrivances failed. The spirit of disaffection soon became apparent, through the grumbling tone assumed by some of the elder lads. Anxious to find a pretext, one or two of the number pulled out short pipes and began to smoke in contravention of the rules, and on doing so they were remonstrated with by the discipline master. This was on Thursday last.

The storm which had been brewing threatened to draw down vengeance on the devoted heads of the officials. The lads John Glennon and John MacNamara were requested to give up their pipes and refused to do so. One or two of the persons in authority – Brown the discipline master, and Tomkins, the overlooker of the work, began to search them. In doing so the youths who formerly were awkward in their manner became obstreperous and violent in their behaviour. Glennon, in a rage, made an attack upon Tomkins, cut his lip and knocked one of his teeth out. The Superior (Father Roberts) desired the offenders to desist but they refused. It was thought advisable that the guilty parties should be put into the cells, but a regular mutiny being apprehended the assistance of the police was considered necessary. A messenger was despatched to Whitwick, and Police Constable Thomas Challoner, proceeded to the establishment. The guardians of the peace at Coalville were also informed of the affray and were soon on the spot, and although it was eight o'clock in the evening, the consternation in the neighbourhood was great and many of the roads busy. When Challoner arrived the lads had returned to their dormitories. These rooms are of considerable size and the upper one is reached by a staircase from the floor of the lower. Each contains about 40 iron bedsteads ranged in four parallel rows along nearly the entire length of the apartment. The pallets are furnished with mattress, sheets, blanket and coverlet and are made to accommodate one person. The policemen proceeded upstairs accompanied by Father Roberts, the rest of the staff connected with the Institution being behind. They passed through the lower dormitory safely. On reaching the upper room the superior called out for Glennon and MacNamara to come quietly out of their beds. The two youths referred to rose up in bed and got out when it was perceived that they were partly dressed and wore their clog shoes. Using foul expressions they cried out to one policeman to "Come on". It was then seen that they were armed with iron bars about two feet long and five eighths of an inch in thickness. The plot was then unveiled. A lot of their confederates sprang out of bed after their chiefs and strengthened with the like weapons which they had prepared by twisting their bedsteads to pieces, they bade the civil authorities defiance. Father Roberts they respected on account of his sacred office but not deeming the police constables function as entitled to the same regard they charged upon him in the most furious and fearful way and bade fair to tear him limb from limb. The starting up of the lads from their beds armed with these implements was like the un-masking of a battery. The police officer's hat was knocked off, he was dragged by his coat shirts and battered with the iron clubs or weapons in the possession of his antagonists. Foremost amongst the aggressors were Glennon and MacNamara; most prominent amongst the rest of the party being Thomas Hughes, Joseph Green and Joseph Shields, and the whole body of elder lads. Challoner stood his ground, drew his staff and defended himself in the best manner possible. Many of the lads got round him; others got on the beds ready for a dash and there was a loud cry for the gas to be extinguished. One of the party – who, it was impossible to tell in the uproar, - aimed a scientific blow at the constable's wrist in order to disable him. He however, failed in his object. The weapon struck Challoner above the wrist and though it hurt him very much, did not prevent him from dealing prompt and vigorous punishment to the army of young rebels before him. A number were knocked down on either side of the room by the policemen and several received cuts and bruises. One or two are now confined to their beds on account of the disastrous effects of the conflict. The melee continued with unabated energy. The policeman, perceiving that the lads were about to make a combined attack, called out for the officers of the establishment, who were in the dormitory below to come and assist him. Father Roberts went to the top of the stairs to call upon his brethren. At that point the rebels simultaneously rushed upon Challoner and Glennon, who was foremost, dealt the constable a sharp and heavy blow on the right side of the head with an iron bar two feet long and nearly an inch in thickness. The policeman was stunned, staggered and retreated. The wound thus inflicted was two inches and a quarter long and rather deep. The blood flowed copiously and it was considered advisable that he should be taken downstairs. His head having been attended to, he inquired of Father Roberts how it was that he did not assist and the reverend gentleman said that it was against his creed to fight. He then sent to Whitwick for more assistance, and Sergeant Peberdy being from home, a number of persons went over from that place to serve if required. Many were requested by Challoner in the Queen's name to help him in the emergency. Being determined to take as prisoners the lads who had first assaulted him it was agreed about 12 o'clock at night to re-enter the upper dormitory for that purpose. The special constables were marshalled and Kelley, (sic) the constable of the place, joined the party. Headed by Challoner they proceeded upstairs. Having reached the lower dormitory they opened the door to ascend to the upper one. The persons occupying the top apartment can, if they choose, look over the stair rails and perceive who is coming up. It happened that the refractory inmates were on the alert, no doubt fancying that there would be a second attempt to apprehend them. They had taken up their position on the top of the stairs in rank, and were not only armed with iron bars, but one or two of them with daggers newly sharpened, which it is supposed the blacksmith had surreptitiously manufactured, whilst the rest were provided with two huge tubs or buckets which in these establishments serve a general purpose and contained on the evening referred to about four or five gallons of urine.

An attempt had been made to uproot the bedsteads, with the intention of throwing them en masse upon any body of persons threatening to come up the staircase to invade the upper dormitory. This had failed owing to the secure way in which the bedsteads were fastened to the floor and to each other. Had it succeeded some would have been massacred. As it was the consequences were serious; the attitude of the enemy alarming. When the stairs door was opened, threatening language was heard from the lads occupying the heights above, as to what they would do, and the iron bars were flourished.

Nothing daunted, however, the party proceeded. As soon as they had got two or three steps up the flight of stairs, they were met, not only with a torrent of abuse, but with a torrent of urine &ct poured forth from the receptacles used in the sleeping apartments. The policeman jumped down to avoid the unpleasant contents of these refuse pans; the rest of the persons, not quite so much alive to the trick, met with a dose of the most unrelishable kind. This interlude did not, however, damp the courage of Challoner and his followers. They recovered themselves as best they could, and boldly marched up. Here the combatants met, and a hand to hand fight took place. The policeman got another blow on the left side of his head; and the constable of the house, named Kelley, received a tremendous cut with a blunt iron instrument on the top of his head. He reeled against the wall, suffused with blood, and in a sinking state, and was taken away. The poor fellow, who bears an excellent character, and who is known by the inoffensiveness of his disposition, was thought at first to be in a hopeless condition: he is now a little better, and it is expected that he will recover. The host of lads were driven from the staircase to the further end of the room, after a hard battle in which many were hurt, and, eventually, five of the number, named John Glennon, John MacNamara, Thomas Hughes, Joseph Green, and Joseph Shields, who could be sworn to as having assaulted Challoner in the first instance, were apprehended. These lads have been sent to the Reformatory from Manchester and Liverpool, and are from 16 to 20 years of age. The police from Coalville having arrived they were all overpowered and taken into custody. They appeared before the magistrates at Ashby on Saturday, and remanded for a week, in order to get further evidence – (that of Kelley, if possible) – and to give time to communicate with the authorities. The lads said that they had made up their minds to escape during the night. A subsequent examination of the building showed that the beds had been broken to pieces, and that there was all the appearance of a united effort on the part of the criminals to crush the "powers that be". The iron bars and daggers, which formed the principal weapons, have been secured. The prisoners who were the ringleaders are locked up. Some of the sufferers have partly recovered, and others yet ill in bed. Mr. Sandford, surgeon, of Whitwick, attended Challoner, and bandaged his head. The inhabitants of the neighbouring towns and villages have been thrown into a state of great consternation by the revolt, and it is supposed that on the representation of the case to the Home Secretary, an investigation will take place. The lads displayed the greatest hardness and daring throughout, and even before the magistrates, seemed to defy their jurisdiction and power.

We subjoin the particulars of the case so far as they have been given in evidence by one witness. As we have remarked, the prisoners were brought up at Ashby on Saturday charged with having assaulted P.C. Challoner, whilst in the execution of his duty on the 8th inst. Their names were given as John Glennon, Thomas Hughes, John MacNamara, Joseph Shields, and Joseph Green. On the bench were Messrs. W.W. Abney (Chairman) T. Mowbray, and R.K. Smith, Esqrs. Challoner, the police officer, on being sworn said, - I am stationed at Whitwick. On Thursday evening last, about eight o'clock, I was sent for by Father Roberts to go to the Reformatory of Mount St. Bernard. When I got there I saw the manager, who told me that Glennon and MacNamara had been misconducting themselves by smoking contrary to the rules. They had been requested to give up their pipes but refused. There was then a scuffle with them and the officers of the establishment tried to take the pipes away. Glennon struck one named Tomkins on the mouth, knocking some of his teeth out, and he wanted me to assist in putting them into the cells. They were supposed to be in bed at this time. I went to the dormitories with Father Roberts and four assistants. They stood at the bottom of the stairs to be ready if required. When I got into the room, Father Roberts called out for Glennon and MacNamara to come out of bed. Glennon immediately jumped out, nearly dressed, having on all his clothes but his coat. Several lads also jumped out, similarly dressed, with their boots on, amongst whom were the three other prisoners, each armed with an iron bar about two feet long, and upwards of an inch thick, being parts of the bedsteads which they had broken up. I said to Glennon "Come out quietly". He made use of some filthy expression, and called to the others to come and assist him. They all rushed forward upon me, and commenced striking. I drew my staff, and defended myself as well as I could. They struck me first on the arm. Glennon got on to a bed and they all made a simultaneous rush at me. Glennon struck me a heavy blow on the right side of the head. I was immediately stunned, and covered with blood. I had previously called out for help, but no-one came. I found none of the others except Father Roberts had come into the room, which was in a perfect uproar. There were about 40 beds in the room. The lads kept shouting out to put the gas out. I had my head bandaged up by the doctor. I asked Father Roberts why he did not assist me and he said it was against their creed to fight. I sent to Whitwick for more assistance. Sergeant Peberdy was from home, but some persons from Whitwick came to my assistance. I returned with the officers of the establishment, and the other assistance I had obtained, being determined to take those out that had assaulted me. When we got to the bottom of the stairs, the five prisoners and some more of the lads, armed as before, stood in rank at the top of the stairs. Some of them called out "Come on". Two of the officers with me attempted to ascend, the others following. When we got part of the way up, they emptied a bucket of night-soil over us, and then threw the bucket. We rushed up to the top of the stairs. Kelly, (the constable of the Reformatory) was heavily struck on the head, and was nearly killed. I was again struck on the left side of my head. Others assisted me, and there was a regular fight. We drove the lads to the other end of the room. Some threw their pieces of iron away, and others (as many as could) jumped into bed with their clothes on. I took the iron from Glennon. The others threw their iron bars down. I apprehended the five prisoners, and brought them to Ashby. Five others were also put into the cell. The prisoners said on the way to Ashby that they all meant to be off before morning, and that all the officers in the place could not take three of them. I went up the next morning with Inspector Ward, when we found eight or nine of the iron bedsteads broken, and others were much damaged. The bars used – of which there were upwards of twenty in court – were principally the legs and tops of the bedsteads. It appears that there was a plot to make their escape before morning. The lads displayed the utmost indifference during the above recital; constantly laughing as the officer proceeded, evidently pleased with the recollection of the share they had in the affray."

It was because of these outbreaks of trouble, reported in the national newspapers, that the Colony became so widely known throughout England and, gradually, there seemed to be a change of attitude from the admiration of the 'noble and selfless' efforts to reform the young criminals to a condemnation of the youths themselves and a perceived need that it was punishment that was required, and that reformation was too high an ideal to hope for.

The Press invariably gave graphic accounts of the misdemeanours of the boys and, in part, there is a familiar ring to the reporting. (2)

"A policeman who has any regard for the dignity of his office is chary of an encounter with the juvenile population. "The London Boy" is a privileged scamp – up to a certain point. But it is possible for boyish outlawry to be pushed a little too far. There is a wide difference between the gamesome tricks of a merely light-hearted youngster and the mischievous vice of an incorrigible young scoundrel. Modern practice allows a good deal of licence to "the boys" but when sport degenerates into vice and borders upon crime, the fun is at an end, and the question becomes serious. Experience shows that vicious lads are dangerous characters. Such are the young scamps who pelt stones at drivers and stokers on railway engines, to the peril of life and limb, and perhaps to the jeopardy of the entire train. Various are the freaks of juvenile iniquity. An old man was once beaten to death by a gang of boys because he would not permit them to pull down his fence for the purpose of making a bonfire wherewith to burn their "guy". For some time past several suburban thoroughfares of London have been infested by troops of disorderly lads particularly on Sunday evenings, and respectable persons have been subject to serious annoyance from their wanton assaults. In past years impertinent boyhood even invaded the precincts of Royalty, and the sentry at the Palace gates………"

infuriatingly that section of the newspaper clipping ends there but appears to be the first column of an editorial which continues with an account of the *"desperate encounter which took place between the banditti of St. Bernard and a small party of bricklayers and their labourers, who may, perhaps, be styled the "Royal Troops" on this occasion."*

This report records a 'break-out' of about fifty boys who came into conflict with the workers but subsequently returned of their own accord to the Reformatory where *'anarchy still reigned'* with the boys apparently in control of the Colony. The writer continues

"On the following day, the lads being at work in a field (they ought every one of them to have been under lock and key, on bread and water), a farmer passed by who had opposed their proceedings the day before. Thirty of the boys immediately conceived the idea of "punishing" the honest farmer, who forthwith had to run as if for his life, and take refuge in an adjacent inn. The audacity of the embryo brigands was evidently a plant of rapid growth. They had the impudence to demand the extradition of the refugee, and being met with a refusal on the part of the landlord, a state of siege resulted –as an attempt was made to storm the house, the windows were smashed, and some of the inmates judged it prudent to take refuge in the cellars. Happily the son of the landlord succeeded in escaping, and brought the police down upon the besiegers, who thereupon fled, six of their number being captured and subsequently sentenced to 14 days hard labour – a punishment which seems altogether inadequate to the offence."

On June 4 1864 in a letter to The Times, William Harper of the Salford Committee played down the event and emphasised that his committee had had control of the Reformatory for ten months only and had been hampered by being obliged to retain 150 boys from the previous management. These boys were "unruly and difficult subjects" but the consequences of that outbreak was that while the offenders were being punished with varying degrees of severity and to prevent any further disturbance it was necessary to retain six policemen on duty within the Reformatory until order was completely restored and this provided an additional expense to the new management.

There followed on June 5 1864 in the Loughborough Monitor a strong rebuttal of the report from the Rev. Thomas Quick, Manager of the Reformatory, who gave a less inflammatory version of the event and said that the

> "real reason [for the boys' assault on the Forest Rock public house] that animated them was a personal antipathy for Castledine who lived there, and who had been, a short time before, employed in the tailor's department, where he had contrived somehow to make himself obnoxious to them."

The Editor acknowledges that had this been at a Protestant reformatory, it would have merited only a couple of lines of newsprint.

THE LATE RIOT AT THE MOUNT ST. BERNARD REFORMATORY.—THE ATTACK ON THE "ROOK INN."

As a result of this riot questions were asked both in the House of Commons by the M.P. for Loughborough, Mr. Packe and in the House of Lords by Lord Berners who quoted the magistrates at Ashby who said that local residents were terrified and that

> "*every decent person in the neighbourhood would sign a petition for the removal of the Reformatory*" because "*neither property nor person was safe when these young ruffians chose to have an outbreak*". (3)

and Lord Berners asked that the Reformatory's certificate be withdrawn. The Secretary of State, Sir George Grey, refused to do this on the recommendation of Sydney Turner, the Home Office Inspector for Reformatories, who had reported to him and had focussed on the cause of the disturbance rather than the details of the occurrence and had found that it was a *"transient and incidental impulse"* which was unlikely to be repeated owing to the improved nature of the management of the Reformatory. However, during these debates and questions Thomas Quick was alleged to be too mild and gentle to have control over the boys and the Salford Committee reluctantly had to ask for his resignation.

The period of calm under the skilful management of Thomas Carroll has already been touched upon in an earlier chapter but the attempts to establish his own mark upon the discipline of the Reformatory by Father Ryan of the Rosminians in 1875 resulted in another riot within months of him taking over the management from Mr. Carroll.
The story in all its graphic details was once again reported in the local press.

"Source: Leicester Journal
Date: 19th November 1875

MOUNT ST. BERNARD'S REFORMATORY.- MUTINY OF THE BOYS

The police have succeeded in recapturing the whole of the youths who mutinied and broke out of the Roman Catholic Reformatory known as the Agricultural Colony of Mount St. Bernard, on Saturday evening. There can be no doubt, from the manner in which this outbreak was carried out, that all the arrangements had been for some time in preparation, and that everything was well arranged by the ringleaders. It is stated that for some time past a strong feeling of disaffection has existed against the new governor of the reformatory, owing to his determination to carry out a more stringent discipline than that which had hitherto prevailed, and which led to a determination on the part of the elder boys to effect their escape, while the younger boys were coerced to join them under the threat of being thrown out of the windows. Saturday night also appears to have been the time fixed upon for the mutiny, as being the night on which there are but few attendants at the institution, through the teachers of trades having finished their week's work and returned to their houses in the neighbourhood. At six o'clock on Saturday evening the supper bell rang as usual, and the whole of the lads, numbering over 100 attended, and betrayed nothing in their demeanour to cause the slightest suspicion, but in the meantime some of the younger boys gave a slight intimation to their attendants (who were at the time only two in number) of what was about to take place. After supper it is usual to form the boys into batches and then march them off to prayers and then to the chapel previous to going to bed, but on Saturday night the keepers deviated from the rule, knowing the plot, and first marched the younger boys straight away to the chapel, and a second lot of older boys was being led off when the ringleaders, finding their movements were being anticipated, uttered a yell, the signal of the outbreak, and the whole institution was in a instant in revolt. The older lads went to the coal-yard, where with a pickaxe they broke up the coal, with which the (sic) pelted the attendants, who terror stricken, and remembering the fearful rows that have previously occurred at the place, betook themselves to their rooms and locked themselves in, while some made all possible haste to Whitwick for assistance. In the meantime the ringleaders broke open the cells in which refractory youths had been confined, and by threats, and it is said in some instances pulling unwilling lads out of the windows, succeeded in getting the whole of the youths, numbering over 100, excepting those confined in the hospital, to join them in making their escape. They then broke into the wash-house, the door of which they demolished, and got out of the window into the garden, from which they got on the drying ground, and from thence over a low wall into the Leicester Forest. In the open they formed themselves into gangs, each taking different directions, but one lot of about thirty, after getting freed from the ringleaders, relented, and returned to the Reformatory, where they were re-admitted about an hour after. The remainder were recaptured in various parts of the County during Sunday, and most singular to state, within twenty-four hours of the outbreak and without one being missing. Most of them were in a miserably wet condition, and one of the youths captured near Leicester had a narrow escape of losing his life by the floods. When approaching Leicester from Groby he had to wade up to the neck through a stream which crossed the road, and was so strong that it carried him off his feet, and would have washed him away but for his becoming entangled in a hedge top, which stopped his downward course and subsequently enabled him to regain his footing on the road. On Monday, the mutineers were summarily dealt with by the Reformatory authorities, being awarded various degrees of punishment, the majority being soundly birched."

No doubt the dreadful conditions experienced by the boys in pursuit of their freedom were the talk of the inmates and probably embellished in the telling and for another two years the Inspector's reports on the Reformatory praised the improvement in behaviour and management, Mr. McCarthy being mentioned particularly for his work on behalf of the boys. But there was to be one final outbreak and in July 1878 when the boys were all gathered on the playground on a Sunday afternoon, the master on duty was suddenly and unexpectedly attacked by some of the boys. About sixty of them made a break together and ran off in a body towards Loughborough but Father Ryan was able to warn the constable in Shepshed who rapidly sent a warning to the police in Loughborough. When the boys had covered the six miles towards the town they must have been surprised and frustrated to find their way blocked by a large number of police and volunteers and a street fight developed between the two parties. The Reformatory boys were no match for the adults who confronted them and most were detained and returned to the Reformatory but there were eight who managed to evade capture, cross the River Soar and vanish into the surrounding countryside, presumably returning to their families by various means in due course.

The Home Secretary ordered an inquiry into the cause of the outbreak and the Inspector's findings blamed the regime of strict punishment and the fact that the building itself was a contributory factor in that it offered opportunities for the boys to conceal themselves and avoid supervision, so it was ordered that a large wall be built around the whole of the Reformatory the better to contain the boys but this was to prove too costly a task and the managers had to relinquish the certificate and close the school on 30 June 1881. The drama of these riotous years was concluded by the 'setting free' of the remaining inmates and those final days of explanation to the boys and their leave-taking can only be imagined.

NOTES

1. Burder letter 22 4 1857 MSBA Archives
2. Press Cuttings Book June 1864 MSBA Archives
3. Press Cuttings Book 21 6 1864

†

OF YOUR CHARITY
PRAY FOR THE SOULS
OF FORTY-TWO
BOYS AND SERVANTS
OF THE REFORMATORY
MOUNT ST BERNARD
WHO DIED BETWEEN
1857 AND 1881 R.I.P.

Chapter 7

DEATHS

The graveyard used by the Reformatory is still evident, marked with a large wooden cross though not with headstones or the usual accoutrements of a cemetery. It is a lonely, quiet enclosure despite the proximity of the traffic on the nearby road and at one time a wooden notice board asked for the public's prayers for the forty two persons who had died at the Reformatory.

Local rumour suggests an outbreak of diphtheria or measles to account for the number of deaths but there has been no evidence of such in the various sources researched over the years. The highest number of deaths recorded in one year is in 1862, when four boys died; Thomas Corcoran (aged 12) died on 22 April from typhoid pneumonia; William Mordan (aged 18) on 11 May from Typhoid fever; James Rigby (aged 15) on 31 May from congestive fever and Patrick Lawless (aged 21) on 9 June from pneumonia and typhus fever. These may be the foundation of the rumour and would certainly be a cause for concern and comment when the death of four inmates was reported in less than two months. Only recently have accounts of individual deaths come to light and some death certificates obtained but most of the forty two are un-named and un-recorded except in the various reports remaining which incidentally state '2 deaths this year' or similar words. *(This changed in 2006; see Appendix)* Mention has already been made of the four who went to America and were killed in the Civil War; we know merely that another was drowned but these would not be among those for whom the public were urged to pray. In the nineteenth century public preoccupation with reformatories it was alleged that the Roman Catholic reformatories had a greater number of boys dying in their care than the Protestant reformatories, the implication being that there was a lack of care and while superficial statistics may have supported the numerical theory, when examined more closely the ratio of deaths was about the same. It was also crucial to the argument that the number of children passing through the Catholic reformatories was far greater than the Protestant reformatories and that their physical condition on conviction was poor because of the background they had, coming in the main from impoverished families.

Henry Kelly was only 15 years old when he committed suicide in July 1858. He had been at the Colony for just over a year having been sentenced to a period of detention of five years by the Liverpool magistrates. His 'crime' is not known. From the evidence given at his inquest it would appear that Henry was a boy who was placed in the wrong sort of care. When he arrived at the Reformatory his head *'was enveloped in bandages'* and on examination it was *'found that the whole crown of his head* [was] *in an ulcerated state'* which the surgeon could not explain. Later, Kelly told some of the other boys that his head injuries were self inflicted to cause the ulceration,

> *"in order to produce some disease of the brain, or as he termed it, lunacy, in order that he might be sent to a reformatory school".* (1)

What his home circumstances were or his fears about the alternative to a reformatory cannot be known but another witness at the inquest said that he thought the deceased was a regular sleepwalker and not in his right mind. This is one of the children who live on in local knowledge today as the ones who were buried beyond the cemetery wall in unconsecrated ground and there is a note in the Abbey archives of an uncorroborated verbal testimony that after Henry's burial, two of the Reformatory boys went out at night and started digging in the grave to retrieve the lad's knife and tobacco tin which had been buried with him. They were spotted by two women who informed the staff and one of the Brothers hastily covered the grave with a large pile of stones.

With youngsters working with farm equipment, animals and maintenance of buildings, accidents were bound to happen but fortunately, there is only one record found so far where an accident resulted in death. Sixteen years old Thomas Jones was working with a Mr. Petch who was operating a steam threshing machine when he was pulled into the machine by a rope he was holding in his hand. The machine was quickly stopped but Thomas sustained injuries to his arm and scalp from which he soon died. (2) A reading of the newspapers of the time quickly reveal that he was not the only young person to fall foul of working machinery.

Another incident which had disastrous consequences occurred in March 1870 when tempers became frayed in the tailor's workshop. Francis McEwan aged 12 made his dying declaration;

> *"I, Francis McEwan, believing I shall die, make this statement of the occurrence which took place on Thursday last. I was working in the tailor's shop under Lawlor. He gave me a waistcoat and said "Sew this up". He said "You b....., you are not doing it right." And struck me on the head with the scissors. He then threw the scissors at me as I jumped out of the way fearing he would again strike me. He then struck me on the head with the scissors and I told him that my bowels were coming out. He then said "Oh, don't tell" and carried me up to the Infirmary. I don't believe he meant to injure me seriously. He was often in a bad temper with me."*

He died two hours later. The surgeon, Mr. Wood, described to the Coroner the abdominal wound he had seen when first called and his attempts to return the intestines to their proper place after administering chloroform to Francis. Initially, Francis seemed to make progress but deteriorated during the following day, dying at midnight. Lawlor was committed to the Assizes on a charge of manslaughter.(3)

The most widely reported death is that of Father Lawrence, whose story was told in Household Words by Charles Dickens' reporter. The article was to describe the celebration of Christmas at the monastery and contained a detailed description of the journey and the travelling from 'Buffborough' (4) across the Forest to the monastery and of the reporter's first impressions of his monastic room and the silence that pervaded but again, it is better to leave the telling of that tale to the original words.

> "……..*we drive through a private gate along a path where the evergreens form a continuous arch above our heads – when I catch a glimpse of a huge mass of rock surmounted by a tall cross – when we finally draw up before a heavy Gothic building, in the large porch of which stands a monk, a bona fide monk, with close cropped hair, long white flannel robe and cowl, dark scapulary, and all monastic appurtenances fitting. He welcomes me warmly, offers me refreshment, and then, ushering me to my bedroom, leaves me to get rid of the dust accumulated in the journey…………*
>
> *A tap at the door rouses me from my reverie, and, opening it, I find my friend the monk outside. He is the guest-master, by name Father Lawrence, the only member of the community, besides the abbot and the prior, on whom the vow of perpetual silence is not binding.*
>
> *I have never seen a sweeter expression of face, slightly worn, slight ascetic, but when he smiles his grey eyes light up, his white teeth gleam, and he is the embodiment of good humour. Again he proffers refreshment, and on my again declining it proposes that we should set out to the reformatory, where a service is about to be performed by the abbot. Of course I agree, and we start. I have on a heavy night-cot, which has seen much rough work, but my companion makes no addition to his dress beyond pulling his cowl over his head; he tells me that custom had rendered him indifferent to cold, and, lantern in hand, he tramps manfully over the stiff furrows of a ploughed field, and through lakelets of standing water.*
>
> *A quarter of an hour's walking on the father's part, and a quarter of an hour's feeble struggling on mine, brings us to the reformatory, where are two hundred Roman Catholic boys, all of whom have been criminally convicted, and are here passing the term of their imprisonment in being educated and taught the means of earning a livelihood instead of, as in old times, consorting with Thomas Idle and his comrades, and envying the exploits of Captain Macheath. Games are going on as we enter, and the large court-yard is ringing with merriment; but no sooner are we perceived than the game is broken up, and, with loud shouts, all the players rush towards my companion, pressing round him, calling out his name, seizing his hand,*

literally striving to "touch the hem of his garment"; never have I seen such enthusiasm and affection! They are only brought back to reason by the sound of a bell, and the warning voices of the monitors calling upon them to "fall in!" in regular military order, and to march up to their chapel, some five minutes distant.

Father Lawrence and I bring up the rear of the long procession. As we walk, he tells me of the success of the institution; how they have never yet failed in any of the cases entrusted to them; how, when the boys are first brought over in charge of the policeman immediately after their sentence, they look upon the removal of the handcuffs as the primary recognition of their human condition; how, from that time forth, day by day they soften and humanise. This reformatory is the father's hobby, that is easily seen, as he talks of it his eyes glisten, and his gestures become more and more animated. Here, he tells me, he spends every spare moment of his life, and here, among those boys, for whose good he has laboured, he would wish to die. He is especially excited tonight, for, at his own cost – or rather, at the cost of his friends, for these monks renounce all separate fortune, and have but one common purse – he has presented the boys' chapel with a new and splendid image of the Virgin Mary, which the abbot is to consecrate at the ensuing service, and he begs me to press forward, that we may be in time for the ceremony.

When we arrive at the chapel – a large plain building, with a railed off altar at the far end, and a vestuary immediately inside the entrance door – we find every seat filled by the boys, but my conductor having been whispered to by a lay brother in attendance, tells me that the abbot wishes to speak to me, and leads me to the robing-room. I am somewhat taken aback on finding my hand cordially shaken by a middle-aged, stout, genial gentleman, who warmly welcomes me, deplores the bad weather, hopes I had a pleasant journey, and who, but for his dress, might be a country member of the Conservative Club whom I have come to visit for a week's shooting.

The service is ended, the boys have returned in procession to their playground, and I am standing by Father Lawrence, inquiring into various details of the place, when he suddenly staggers and recovers himself by grasping my shoulder. A little boy to whom he had been speaking is advancing towards him, and I imagine that this sudden movement is mere playfulness on *his part directed towards the child, when, on glancing at him, I perceive that his face is deadly white; I ask him if he feels faint, and he replies, endeavouring to smile, " I have a curious sensation which I never had before. You must excuse me for —-". That sentence is never finished; those words are the last that the thin lips ever frame! He reels as he speaks and falls heavily into my arms. I catch him and bear him to the nearest room – the kitchen- where I lay him on a long wooden dresser and summon help. A few persons come at my call; the prior, two or three lay brothers, and finally an old monk, who is supposed to have some knowledge of medicine. A death-like pallor has come over the face of the stricken man; his lips are blue; his mouth is set and rigid; the old monk loosens his gown, chafes his hands and temples, gives me one rapid and meaning look; a minute afterwards the prediction contained in that glance is fulfilled, and Father Lawrence is dead! An hour since, and he was expressing his hope that he should die amongst the boys; now, the hum and bustle of the playground swell upon us as, lying in the midst of us, he passes Out of the World."*

Father Lawrence Hairby

John Hannon's death was publicised in a lesser fashion but, at least, he was one of the few boys awarded lasting remembrance in the annals of the Colony. Abbot Burder described his brief life and death in a letter to the press on Sunday of Easter Week, 1858.

"Dear Sir,
All will agree that Easter Week is a beautiful time for the young to die – for those, at least, among the young of whom we have the consoling hope that they "die in the Lord". It is a holy time, when the Church is keeping the greatest of her Feasts – the time, too, of looking forward to the future resurrection of the glorified body – it is the spring time, the time of coming again of field flowers, and the singing again of the birds, and the rising again of all joyful things from their winter graves. This Easter Week, moreover, is the latter part of the time of Jubilee; therefore it is a doubly happy time. This is the week that Our Lord chose for the death and burial of one of our dear-boys at the Colony – the first we have lost by death – or rather the first of our 300 young penitents who has gone to a "better land", as we confidently hope, and reached in safety the shore of a happy eternity. It is a happy thing for me to have to record his holy death, and his blameless life since he first became an inmate of St. Mary's Colony. May I be allowed to mention a few particulars about him – as they may gratify some of your readers who, I know, take the deepest interest in this great work of love:- John Hannon was admitted to the Colony in February 1857. He was fifteen years of age. He came from Liverpool. His father was dead. His mother, poor woman, could hardly gain for herself the scantiest existence. John became a tenant of the streets. For five years he had been accustomed to frequent the Docks, trying to get there his chance of work. There he fell, and a great and bad fall it was, into the company of other boys who led him astray. He began to lead an idle and loose life. Poor boy, he soon went on to steal. He was taken up by the police, convicted, and sentenced, after a short imprisonment, to be detained five years in St. Mary's Colony. "O felix culpa! – Oh happy fault, which was the occasion of John's coming to the Colony!" His conduct in the Colony, from the first, was good. He was regular in attending punctually all the Colony exercises, particularly in getting up in the morning directly he heard the warning sound, the clap of the hands, and the "Benedicamus Domino – Let us bless the Lord". He was also very exact in saying his morning and night prayers, and especially in reciting the prayer of the Angelus, which seemed to please him much.
A few weeks ago, the Brother at whose table John sat observed

that he did not take his meals well. On being asked how he was, he said he felt very weak and had no appetite; and then, with tears, he asked permission to be removed from the company of the other boys, as he could not join in their exercises nor in their play. The permission was granted, and John began immediately to prepare himself for death. He was in a rapid consumption. He often expressed a wish to die, if it would be pleasing to God. He begged me to invest him with the Brown Scapular of Our Lady of Mount Carmel, which I did, a fortnight before his death. He was very particular in getting the good boy who attended him to recite every day the prayers attached to this devotion. He had his Rosary either on his person or close to him, his Agnus Dei, and his blessed Medal of St. Benedict, and also a small Crucifix, blessed by the Holy Father with a Plenary Indulgence at the hour of death. The kisses John used to give these holy things were very earnest and audible ones, full of love and faith. He suffered great pains, being of a strong frame, but he bore them with great patience. I was much consoled to observe, during the last two weeks before his death, that his countenance lost a rather sad and worn expression it used to have, and that it put on a constant smile, a calm and sweet look, which seemed to make known the happy state of his mind and heart and conscience: May Our Lord be praised for His goodness! When he thought he was alone, he used to invoke, with great fervour, the holy names Jesus, Mary and Joseph; and his other favourite aspiration was, "My Jesus, I do this for love of you", which the boys at the Colony are taught to say before they begin any work. John often asked to be sprinkled with holy water, and was very grateful to anyone who said any Litanies or prayers by his bedside. He received the Last Sacraments with edifying devotion, keeping his hand lifted up in prayer.......The only thing which seemed to trouble him was that he could not assist his poor widowed mother.

The good Chaplain of the Colony heard John's last confession a very short time before he died; and after his confession John spoke of the great peace and contentment he felt in his mind. Soon after, he quietly breathed his last breath, and, assisted by his Guardian Angel, fell asleep in Our Lord, during the recitation of Our Blessed Lady's Litany. "Resquiescat in pace". I was not present when he died, but I soon heard of his happy end; and I need not say how fervently I thanked the Adorable Trinity for having, in a short illness of three weeks, so purified the soul of this good boy, and prepared it for glory.........
When he was laid out in white so prettily by the Brothers, in the room in which he died, the boys kept constantly coming in, by

> turns, to say prayers for the repose of his soul. I came suddenly into the room the day after his death, and a beautiful sight indeed I saw, which must have rejoiced, I think the Holy Angels. There was John, dressed in white, in the centre of the room, lying on his humble bier, the hands crossed meekly on his breast, a sweet smile on his face, and all his little holy property arranged abut his person – the Rosary, the Scapular, the Agnus Dei, and the favourite Medal. Four candlesticks were about the bier, two at the feet and two at the head; the two at the feet were lighted. By the side of the white body was a group of three little boys kneeling; one of them was reading some prayers as well as he could, and the other two, with hands lifted up and their palms closed, were listening and responding............It was a scene for a holy painter – but there are few such painters now-a-days....Today, Saturday in Easter Week, Hannon was buried in the Colony Garden, among the flowers and trees....."

There is no sense of any personal emotion in Abbot Burder's public story or feeling that the death of a child must be accounted for and we are left to wonder how the parents were informed and if they were given any opportunity to visit their child's burial place. Children were perhaps in those days, more accepting of death but even so, the death of a fellow inmate, a dormitory colleague, a friend, must have caused a great deal of subdued talk amongst the boys.

The old notice board cites the "42 boys and servants" whose deaths occurred at the Reformatory but it is only through the chance discovery of an approximate date that a search can begin for the circumstances of the deaths using the local newspapers of the time. An archive note, *'Death of woman cook at Reformatory'*, led eventually to the report of the Coroner's Inquest in February 1867 on Bridget Owen, aged 38. Bridget, a single woman, was resident at the Colony and had failed to appear for work one morning which was unusual. A lad was sent to her room to find out why and he returned quickly saying that she was dying and that the room was full of gas. Mr. Carroll, then Superintendent, gave evidence that she had been in good health and spirits when he last saw her on the previous evening and that he thought she must have gone to bed by gas-light in preference to candle-light and, somehow, when extinguishing the light, must have accidentally turned the switch again thus allowing gas to escape. The surgeon from Shepshed stayed with her until she died some twenty-four hours later. (5)

Another death is recorded in the Guest Book of 1858-1866 which briefly states;

> "March 28th 1858. Brother Benedict of the Colony departed this life. Interred in the Cemetery on the 30th ".

It was reasonable to assume that Brother Benedict was one of Abbot Burder's Third Order Brothers so it was somewhat of a surprise to find from his death certificate that he was one John Silk, aged 70 years, an Almsman, formerly a Whitesmith, who died from a diseased liver. His story and how he came to the end of his life in a Reformatory exercising supervision over delinquent boys will never be known.

For a twenty-first century person interested in the history of his neighbourhood, the fact that so many young boys were removed from family and friends and committed to spend a formative period of their youth locally, gradually dispersed to take up their new life, or return to the old, is one which warrants investigation simply from an objective point of view, but the knowledge that a percentage of those boys ended their life in circumstances which have been allowed to disappear brings a subjective element into research. Only the cynical could describe as maudlin the need to personalise these deaths and thus achieve, at least, a token memorial for them.

NOTES

1. Press Cuttings Book 6 August 1858. MSBA Archives
2. *Loughborough Monitor* 21 November 1867 Leicestershire Record Office (Hereafter LRO)
3. *Loughborough News* 7 April 1870 LRO
4. 'Loughborough'
5. *Leicester Journal* 22 February 1867 LRO

The last of the Colony 1995

CONCLUSION

The pieces of the Reformatory jigsaw were scattered throughout the country, hard to find and even more difficult to put together and the picture is still incomplete and will probably remain so. The failures of the reformatory were due to a combination of factors and cannot be blamed on Abbot Burder alone. There is no dispute that his intentions were good but he had had no proper formation into Cistercian life and in his personal arrogance he failed to appreciate the enormity and unproven nature of the undertaking. His greatest failure was to his community in failing to communicate, in doing what he wanted without discussion, *'the Abbot's will is everything in the house'*, and refusing to take into account the roots of Cistercian monasticism. The legacy he left the monastery was not only financial disaster but also the continuing need to be involved with subsequent managers, detrimental to the contemplative ideal, and a long period of collective depression as the monks tried to recoup finances, to return to a simple life of Work and Prayer and rebuild a reputation which would attract the necessary new vocations. The monastic community did survive and weathered the very lean years which followed after Abbot Burder's brief period of office, gradually accumulating a wisdom from what had gone before them. After his resignation Burder had further trials to suffer; he asked to be taken in to other monasteries, some admitting him, others refusing, his reputation having gone before him and he eventually died in September 1881 at Lulworth Castle, a place regarded as the birthplace of the monastic foundation at Mount St Bernard Abbey and in the same year that St. Mary's Agricultural Colony closed.

Most of the Colony buildings were allowed to deteriorate though some survived for a hundred years after the last boys left serving as dwellings for a time in the first part of the twentieth century and latterly as a grain and potato store. The site is unrecognisable having been buried under tons of rubble excavated from the path of the M1 Motorway as it carved its way through Charley Parish in the 1950s and is now overgrown with bramble and nettles. The last building standing behind Bath Meadow was demolished in 1995.

The reformatory system settled down during the latter half of the nineteenth century and reformatory schools proliferated, persisting into the twentieth century. They were gradually absorbed into a comprehensive state penal system which on the whole dealt less harshly with juvenile offenders. Only persistent offenders or those convicted of serious crimes were given the severe punishment of removal from their home territory and committal to 'Approved' Schools where it was hoped that the necessary reformation of character would take place.

The boys of St Mary's Agricultural Colony? Well, most of them survived but what became of them is not known. They are the missing pieces of the jig-saw and their adult stories can only be told if the detective work of family historians uncovers the roots of their forefathers and it will be then, in each individual case, that the work of the Colony can be deemed success or failure. The task of family historians is now made easier with access to the National Census records available through the internet and by this means the names of 915 boys and 100 adult members of staff have been found and these are to be kept in the archives of Mount St Bernard Abbey. Edward Shanley whose name began this account of the Reformatory does not appear on the 1871 National Census so what became of him in later life is a story yet to be told.

APPENDIX

It had been possible to obtain death certificates for those whose deaths at the Reformatory had been recorded by name either in the Colony's Annual Reports or in the local newspapers and by these means some twelve certificates were found.

A death certificate records information in a formulaic way which has not changed over the centuries. First there is the registration number, then the date of death, the place of death and there follows details of the deceased and the person providing the information. Until the twentieth century all this was handwritten in permanent ink in huge ledgers held in the individual Registration Districts. In the twelve certificates obtained the place of death was invariable recorded as "The Reformatory Whitwick" but verbal and written request to the Registrars' Office for a more general search was always refused on the grounds that a name was essential as a first point of reference.

During May and June 2006 communications with David Taylor, M.P. for North West Leicestershire about the Freedom of Information Act 2000 brought me in a roundabout way to Mrs. Jill Hall, the Superintendent Registrar for Leicestershire and keeper of the nineteenth century ledgers. Mrs. Hall had been aware of the requests for specific searches through general conversations with her staff and their interest in an element of local history previously unknown to them but she did not appreciate the number of deaths which had occurred at the Reformatory. She too became enthusiastic and agreed that over a period of time, as work commitments allowed, a search could be made of the ledgers using the place of death as a locator. This was exciting news and I expressed a hope that the search could be completed by Christmas 2006.

Within two weeks a telephone call informed me that an additional thirty three recorded deaths had been found and that the certificates were available on payment of the usual fee.

The old notice board asking for prayers for the deceased of the Reformatory stated "Boys and staff" but the certificates revealed personal tragedies for Mr. Thomas Carroll, Governor during the 1860s, and his wife. Their twelve month old son, Thomas, had died in October 1866 from convulsions; Carroll's mother, Ellen died in 1871 aged seventy one years and during the family's brief return from the Garendon Estate they lost a daughter in 1874, also aged one year and again the cause of death was given as convulsions.

Thomas Whitacre was fifteen years old when he died of consumption at the Reformatory in 1865 and was probably not an inmate as his father William Whitacre, a farm labourer, was present at his death and it may be the same family which experienced the loss of another child in 1870 when Thomas William Whittaker aged one year died of pneumonia at the Reformatory Lodge. His father was also William Whittaker, a farm labourer.

The Community of Mount St Bernard Abbey is deeply grateful to the staff of the Registrars' Office for uncovering this information for it now means that the deaths can be acknowledged particularly in the prayer life of the monks.

DEATHS AT THE REFORMATORY, WHITWICK

DATE	NAME	AGE	CAUSE OF DEATH
22 1 1857	John Joseph Connor	19 years	Phithisis (Tuberculosis)
28 3 1858	John Silk	70 years	Diseased liver
8 4 1858	Michael Hannan	17 years	Phithisis
12 6 1858	James Dayley	13 years	Phthisis
28 7 1858	Henry Kelly	16 years	Felo de Se (Suicide)
21 1 1860	John Haddican	14 years	Phthisis Pulmonalis
17 6 1861	John Hanley	16 years	Erysipelas of the head and face
9 1 1862	Edward Power	18 years	Phthisis
5 2 1862	William Smith	19 years	Typhoid Pneumonia
22 4 1862	Thomas Corcoran	12 years	Typhoid Pneumonia
11 5 1862	William Mordan	18 years	Typhoid Fever Pneumonia
16 5 1862	John Illsley	15 years	Pneumonia
31 5 1862	James Rigby	15 years	Congestive Fever
9 6 1862	Patrick Lawless	21 years	Typhus Fever
20 12 1864	Peter Wood	13 years	Phthisis
1 6 1865	Thomas Whitacre	15 years	Consumption
4 10 1866	Thomas Carroll	1 year	Convulsions
15 2 1867	Bridget Owen	38 years	Apoplexy arising from the inhalation of coal gas
23 8 1867	James Doogan	15 years	Peritonitis (post-Mortem)
14 11 1867	Thomas Jones	16 years	Fracture of skull from accidentally falling into a Threshing machine
1 8 1868	John Locke	17 years	Phthisis
16 8 1868	Patrick Noon	12 years	Tabes Mesenterica
26 4 1869	Alfred Cook	11 years	Phthisis and Tabes Mesenterica

DATE	NAME	AGE	CAUSE OF DEATH
29 4 1869	John Lacy	16 years	Peritonitis
11 1 1870	Thomas William Whittaker	1 year	Pneumonia
8 2 1870	Charles McCarthy	16 years	Scrofula Abscess of the Brain
21 3 1870	Patrick O'Connor	16 years	Consumption
27 3 1870	Francis McEwan	12 years	Manslaughter
6 5 1871	Ellen Carroll	71 years	Schirrhus of stomach
24 5 1871	Michael Cain	16 years	Phthisis
14 6 1871	Stephen Woulfe	18 years	Phthisis
22 10 1872	Henry O'Brien	14 years	Phthisis with congestion of Lungs Effusion on the Brain
8 4 1874	John Fitzgerald	14 years	Phthisis
11 6 1874	George Riley	16 years	Phthisis
30 7 1874	John McCormack	14 years	Phthisis
3 8 1874	Edward Keefe	16 years	Fever Sudden Effusion of the Brain
4 8 1874	Margaret Carroll	1 year	Convulsions
16 9 1874	Francis Bernard Wale	8 weeks	Debility from Birth Convulsions
2 6 1875	Thomas Hussey	17 years	Phthisis Pulmonalis
13 2 1876	John Mulligan	14 years	Jaundice; Meningitis
24 12 1876	Thomas McGiffe	14 years	Meningitis Tubercular
28 10 1878	Thomas Spencer	13 years	Cerebral Spinal Meningitis
29 10 1878	Michael Rose	17 years	Cerebro Spinal Meningitis
4 5 1879	Thomas Callaghan	14 years	Phthisis Pulmonalis
19 4 1880	Peter Pheeney	17 years	Morbus Brightii

Phithisis - Usually refers to Tuberculosis of the lungs.
Erysipelas - Type of cellulitis (skin infection)
Tabes Mesenterica - Tuberculosis of the mesenteric and retroperitoneal lymph nodes
Scrofula - Tuberculous infection of the skin of the neck
Schirrhus - Hard tumour / carcinoma
Morbus Brightii - Another name for dropsy or kidney disease

BIBLIOGRAPHY

BECK George Andrew A A Ed   *The English Catholics 1850-1950*   (Burns Oates London 1950)

HOLMES J Derek   *More Roman than Rome: English Catholicism in the Nineteenth Century*   (Burns & Oates London 1978)

HORN Pamela   *The Victorian Town Child*   (Sutton Publishing Ltd Stroud 1997)

TOBIAS J J   *Nineteenth-Century Crime: Prevention and Punishment* (David & Charles Newton Abbot 1972)

SHAW A G L *Convicts & the Colonies. A Study of Penal Transportation from Great Britain and Ireland to Australia and Other Parts of the British Empire* (Faber and Faber 1966 The Irish Historical Press Ltd 1998)

CROCKER John Ed   *Charnwood Forest: A Changing Landscape* Loughborough Naturalists Club   (Sycamore Press 1981)

RADZINOWICZ L and HOOD R *The Emergence of Penal Policy in Victorian and Edwardian England*   (Clarendon Press Oxford 1990)

RADZINOWICZ L *A History of English Criminal Law Vol 1 The Movement for Reform*   (Stevens and Sons Ltd 1948)

RADZINOWICZ L and TURNER J W C Eds   *Penal Reform in England* (Macmillan and Co Ltd 1946 2nd Edition)

CARPENTER M *Reformatory Schools for Children of the Perishing and Dangerous Classes and for Juvenile Offenders* C Gilpin 1851   (Woburn Books 1968)

RIMMER J *Yesterday's Naughty Children – a History of Liverpool's Reformatory Association Founded in 1855*   undated

DESSAIN C S Ed *The Letters and Diaries of J H Newman Vol xi Littlemore to Rome January 1845-December 1846*   (Thomas Nelson and Sons Ltd 1961)

DESSAIN C S Ed *The Letters and Diaries of J H Newman Vol xii Rome to Birmingham January 1847-December 1848*   (Thomas Nelson and Sons Ltd 1961)

McCONVILLE S *English Prisons 1860-1900 Next Only to Death* (Routledge 1995)

PAWLEY M *Faith and Family: the Life and Circle of Ambrose Phillipps de Lisle* (The Canterbury Press 1993)

PURCELL E S *Life and Letters of Ambrose Phillipps de Lisle Vol 1 and 2* (Macmillan and Co 1900)

SHORE H *Artful Dodgers: Youth and Crime in Early Nineteenth Century London* (The Boydell Press 1999)

WILLIAMS D Ed *The Adaptation of Change: Essays Upon the History of Nineteenth Century Leicester and Leicestershire* (Leicester Museums Publication No 18 1980)